Bishop Getties L. Jackson, Sr.
Pastor Anita F. Jackson

So Goes The Man,

So Goes The Family

BY

Bishop
GETTIES L. JACKSON, SR., M. DIV.

Foreword by Bishop Dale C. Bronner

Reflections by Pastor Anita F. Jackson

So Goes The Man, So Goes The Family

FIRST EDITION

Copyright © 2015 Bishop Getties L. Jackson, Sr., M. Div.

ISBN-13:978-1507568750

Ephesians 5:25-28 from the Message Bible reads *"Husbands, go all out in your love for your wives, exactly as Christ did for the church—a love marked by giving, not getting. Christ's love makes the church whole. His words evoke her beauty. Everything he does and says is designed to bring the best out of her, dressing her in dazzling white silk, radiant with holiness. And that is how husbands ought to love their wives. They're really doing themselves a favor—since they're already 'one' in marriage".* What a command from the Lord!

You see husbands, it begins with us! It is about sacrificing for your wife, which will ultimately impact the entire family.

I dedicate this book to my wife of 32 years, Pastor Anita Jackson. She's bone of my bone and flesh of my flesh. She is my best friend, and she's also my greatest investment. As we have journeyed together in ministry for 30 years, it has been a blessing from the Lord. We are truly a testament to the truths and principles that you will read. What is even more exciting is that at the end of each part of this book, Pastor Anita has written a *"Reflection"* of her journey and how that particular part of the book has spoken to her as a woman of God.

God has surrounded me with an awesome team, and I want to thank each one of them for their love, their support, and their dedication to Kingdom business. This work could not have been accomplished without them. Teamwork makes the dream work! I also want to thank God for placing Bishop Dale C. Bronner in my life as my spiritual father in the gospel.

The Old English word "family" literally meant "father's house". That's why the family name was the father's last name. The family is the most basic unit of society. So goes the man, so goes the family. So goes the family, so goes the school, the church, the government, etc. In this book, Bishop Jackson gives clear biblical instructions to help men become better men of God. This in turns helps the family to be better. When the family is better, the society is better.

Sociologist George Gilder in his book <u>Sexual Suicide</u>, makes it clear that single men (as a class) are often a threat to society. Until they accept the responsibility for families, their sexual aggression is largely unbridled and potentially destructive. Gilder writes:

> *"Men commit over 90% of major crimes of violence, 100% of the rapes, [and] 95% of the burglaries. They comprise 94% of drunken drivers, 70% of suicides, [and] 91% of offenders against family and children. Single men comprise between 80 and 90% of most of the categories of social pathology and on the average make less money than any other group in society—yes, less than single women or working women. As any insurance actuary will tell you, single men are also less responsible about their bills, their driving and other personal conduct."*

Fathers are ultimately given responsibility over the seed that they produce. God even gave Adam responsibility of Eve. This is why God went to Adam first after Eve sinned. This is not a put down of women or an attempt to blame. Manhood is about accepting responsibility!

If a marriage fails, the man is ultimately responsible. Fathers are responsible for their children. At the end of the day, our children will remember our CHARACTER rather than our RULES and REGULATIONS!

Years ago, an article in a clergy magazine told of a fictional account of a pastor in a medium-sized church who had a dream one night in which a voice said to him, "There are fifty teenagers in your church. You have the ability to lead forty-nine of them to God and lose out on only one."

Inspired by the dream, the pastor threw himself into youth work with imagination and energy. He taught extra classes for the adolescents in his community. He raised funds to take them on class trips. It worked. The pastor won a national reputation in his denomination for his work with young people.

Then, one night, the pastor discovered that his 16 year old son had been arrested for dealing drugs. The boy had turned bitterly against the church and its teachings, resenting his father for having had time for every 16 year old in town except him, and the father had never noticed.

The pastor's son was the 50th teenager, the one who got away. We cannot afford to lose our children at the expense of business, making money, or even ministry. Let's be the men God has called us to be!

Bishop Dale C. Bronner, Founder/Senior Pastor
Word of Faith Family Worship Cathedral

So Goes The Man . . .

Contents

Part I - *Reaching the Next Level*

1. Your History Does Not Dictate Your Destiny   15
2. Rising to a Higher Level   25
3. Who Are You Hanging With?   37

So Goes the Woman - Pastor Anita F. Jackson   49

Part II - *Walking in Purpose and Destiny*

4. God Wants You in Purpose   55
5. We Have to Train Up Our Children   69
6. God Kept You Alive Because of Destiny Inside   79

So Goes the Woman - Pastor Anita F. Jackson   89

Part III - *Staying Alive*

7. The Fever is Broken   95
8. Three Levels of Relationships   111
9. I Won't Run Out!   121

So Goes the Woman - Pastor Anita F. Jackson   129

Part IV - *A New Creation in Christ*

10. Raise Your Level of Expectation   135
11. You Can't Die, You Must Survive This!   151
12. Get Rid of the Weights!   165

So Goes the Woman - Pastor Anita F. Jackson   173

Notes   179

About the Author   183

Part I

Reaching
the Next Level

Chapter One
Your History Does Not Dictate Your Destiny

Josiah was eight years old when he became king, and he reigned thirty-one years in Jerusalem. And he did what was right in the sight of the Lord, and walked in the ways of his father David; he did not turn aside to the right hand or to the left. For in the eighth year of his reign, while he was still young, he began to seek the God of his father David; and in the twelfth year he began to purge Judah and Jerusalem of the high places, the wooden images, the carved images, and molded images. They broke down the altars of the Baals in his presence, and the incense altars which were above them he cut down; and in the wooden images, the carved images, and molded images he broke in pieces, and made dust of them and scattered it on the graves of those who had sacrificed to them.

2 Chronicles 34:1-4 (NKJV)

Say, "My history does not dictate my destiny." We have all done some things. The Bible does not say, "Ya'll have sinned" but *"all have sinned"* (Refer to Romans 3:23). All includes everybody that has ever lived. All of us have sinned and come short of the glory of God. Now, this is major! Romans 8:28 (KJV) paraphrased, *". . . and we know that He works all things. . ."* Our history then becomes "his story". According to Romans 8:28 (KJV), *"And we know that all things work together for good to them that love God, to them who are the called according to his purpose."*

We are trying to get rid of stuff that's been holding us back. For some it may be a sexual sin that has been handed down generationally. It just didn't start with you; I can assure you. If you have a spirit of lust, if you check in your bloodline, it's going to be there, it's been in your bloodline long before you got here on planet earth. I can assure you. This is real stuff. Never think that it just started with you. This is why we have to break this thing so it doesn't pass on to our children and our grandchildren.

For some of us, it is a mental struggle. We have low self-esteem. We don't have clarity of our assignment. We don't know who we are in Christ. We are always feeling sorry for our self. We have this "me-me-my" syndrome. It is like we're saying, "I don't know why I did that." It is a mental struggle. If you have a mental struggle, learn to meditate on 2 Corinthians 10:4-5 (NKJV), *"For the weapons of our warfare are not carnal but mighty in God for pulling down strongholds, casting down arguments and every high thing that exalts itself against the knowledge of God, bringing every thought into captivity to the obedience of Christ."* For people with low self-esteem, don't say to them, "You shouldn't be feeling that way!" That's how they feel. Why are you fussing at them? You are struggling with something too. Everybody has some kind of struggle. We are not called to humble people but we are called to help people. We have to help each other. We learn from each other.

For some, it may be a marital struggle and for others it may be losing weight. I can assure you, if you are alive, there is a struggle going on. We are not the finished product. I know we have scriptures like 1 Corinthians 2:9 (NKJV), *"Eye has not seen,* nor ear heard, nor have entered into the heart of man the things which God has prepared for those who love Him", and my life verse, Philippians 1:6 (NKJV), *"being confident of this very thing, that He who has begun a good work in you will complete it until the day of Jesus Christ."* Know that God is not through with us yet. To get to the next level, there are some things that you need to tear down and demolish. There are things from our past that has carried over into our present that we need to tear down.

Josiah was the king that reigned over Jerusalem when he was eight years old (Refer to 2 Chronicles 33:1, 21-22). Manasseh is Josiah's grandpa, and Amon is Josiah's daddy. At the end of his life, Manasseh felt sorry about his wrong doings as a king but his daddy didn't care. In other words, his grandpa humbled himself. So, Josiah is eight years old when he became king but his dad and his grandpa were a trip. This eight year old king name Josiah says, "I don't care what my daddy or grandpa did, I'm serving the Lord!" You may be the one that will stand for God if no one else in your family will stand for God. *"In the eighth year of his reign, while he was still young, he began to seek the God of his father David; and in his twelfth year he began to purge Judah and Jerusalem of the high places . . . the Asherah poles and the idols"* (2 Chronicles 34:3 NKJV). It doesn't say that Josiah sought the God of his father or grandfather. David is Josiah's great, great, great grandfather.

Did you know that many of us are living on the prayers of our grandparents? The reason I'm living right is not to get a car, a house, or a new wardrobe, but I want my kids and my grandkids to be blessed. You are not living right just for you. I want you to start thinking generationally and set up trust funds and wills. The reason some ethnicities prosper more than others is because they don't just think about buying a new car every year or two. Instead, think about putting some money up, and get some insurance. Start thinking about your children, and stop trying to show off by buying cars and renting a house.

Under his direction the altars of the Baals were tore down; he cut to pieces the incense altars that were above them, and smashed the Asherah poles and the idols. These he broke to pieces and scattered over the graves of those who had sacrificed to them.

2 Chronicles 34:4 (NIV)

In 2 Chronicles 34:4, King Josiah is just 20 years old. Listen, don't wait until you get old because there will be a lot of regrets. At just 20 years old Josiah is saying, "My daddy and my grandpa did some things that hurt the Kingdom." Josiah tears down every stature of Baal worship, and he wants to rebuild God's Holy City, but he can't rebuild until he demolishes. Let's demolish everything that represents the past sins and ungodliness. Let's make this relevant for us today.

Before you can get to your next level, what is inside of you that represents ungodliness that's still alive but it needs to die? What happened in your life that you think you are over, but you just tucked it away? What is in your life that has a hole in it, but you placed a picture over it? If you are trained as I am, you can see through the picture and see brokenness behind the picture. So, the issue becomes what is hindering me from getting to the next level?

Finally, my brethren, be strong in the Lord and in the power of His might. Put on the whole armor of God, that you may be able to stand against the wiles of the devil.

Ephesians 6:10-11 (NKJV)

Going to Another Level

First, in order to get to the next level **you need to have a different perspective.** Revelation 4:1 says, *"after these things I looked, and behold, a door standing open in heaven, and the first voice which I had heard, like the sound of a trumpet speaking to me, said, 'Come up here, and I will show you what must take place after these things.'"* Christ is talking to John the Revelator, and Christ is saying, "Come up here, and I will show you." The reason God is not talking to some of you is because you need to "come up". When you first got saved, God talked to you on that level. At some point, He got quiet. Maybe the reason why you don't hear God anymore is because He wants you to come up so that He can show you what He really wants to do in your life. You have been with God too long to still be on milk and to be in the same old mess. When you come up, God will give you a new revelation. We have to break stuff that's rooted in us.

I pray that the eyes of your heart may be enlightened, so that you will know what is the hope of His calling, what are the riches of the glory of His inheritance in the saints and what is the surpassing greatness power toward us who believe. These are in accordance with the working of the strength of His might which He brought about in Christ, when He raised Him from the dead and seated Him at His right hand in the heavenly places, far above all rule and authority and power and dominion, and every name that is named, not only in this age but also in the one to come. And He put all things in subjection under His feet, and gave Him as head over all things to the church.

Ephesians 1:18-22

Christ is above your issues! He is above your baby's daddy or baby's momma. Christ is above cancer! If it has a name, it must bow to the name of Jesus. He's above what's been driving you crazy. The devil has been holding you hostage for too long. Let's make a declaration together: No weapon! Stake your claim, and walk in who you are in Christ. So, I have to change my perspective (panoramic view) - looking at it from a different angle. Quit looking at things in the natural. I need some money; look at the spirit behind that. You work two jobs; you are not lazy. You've been working since you were 16 but you are still broke. So, there has to be something behind that. You are paying tithes, and you are living right so maybe this is something deeper than financial. This is a spiritual issue. Maybe this is a generational curse that you never broke. Change your perspective, the way you view things. Most of us call ourselves Christians, but we don't think spiritual - we think natural. We think natural when something jumps off in our life, and we think of our plan to fix it. We don't look at the root of the problem behind it; we treat the symptom. We need to change our perspective, then we need to change our posture, because we've been fighting defensively. Let's stand offensively.

Put on the whole armor of God, that you may be able to stand against the wiles of the devil.

Ephesians 6:11 (NKJV)

While you are asleep, the devil is scheming. While you are in church, the devil has a strategy. If things are going good for you right now, then you had better believe that the devil and his demons are sitting at a table trying to figure out how to get you broke and depressed again. Since the devil is scheming, I cannot play defense only. I need some free agents to play some offense. Defense means preventing the devil, but defense by itself is not enough without any offense. Some people might be waiting on the devil to slap them. Bring your offense, your game to him, and say, "Devil, I know you are trying to hurt me, but I pity you and your demons that are trying to stop me! Devil, I'm going to find 10 scriptures that say I have the victory!"

Not only must I stand offensively, I must stand consistently. I've got to stand consistently because the Bible says that if I allow the demon to come back, he comes back seven times stronger. Ephesians 6:13 (KJV) says, *"Having done all, stand."* Galatians 6:9 (paraphrased), *"Don't you grow weary in your well doing because in due season you will reap what you sow if you faint not."* Learn to stand armed and dangerous. First Corinthians 10:4-

5 (paraphrased) states, *"For the weapons of our warfare are not carnal but mighty through God..."* You have the anointing to break off curses today. I don't care what's in your bloodline, how many people you went to bed with, or how many mistakes you have made. There are some weapons that you have, and if you begin to use these weapons, you will see victory in your life.

Victory Over Your Life

The first weapon is the sword of the spirit, which is the Word of God. The Word of God is an offensive weapon. All of the other weapons used in Ephesians 6 are defensive weapons. When Satan says you are nothing, you say, "I am more than a conqueror through Christ who loves me." There is something you have called "The Blood of Jesus". Maybe you are an old Holy Ghost-filled person or you know of someone because no one talks about the Blood of Jesus anymore. The old spirit-filled mothers would see the devil walking through their house and would stop what they were doing and say, "The Blood of Jesus is against you Satan!" When you see the devil coming against you, you had better learn to stand up and say, "Satan, the Blood of Jesus is against you! I'm bought with a price, and Christ changed my whole life." You may love the song, "What Can Wash Away My Sins". Have you been washed in the Blood of Jesus? Praise God for the Blood of Jesus! The old folks used to say, "The Blood, the Blood will never lose its power!" I want to make a declaration over your life. Decree and declare this:

I decree and declare that the weapons of my warfare are not carnal but mighty through God to the pulling down of strongholds. I cast down every vain imagination and every high thing that exalts itself against the knowledge of God. My thoughts are now subject to the Blood of Jesus Christ. God's anointing destroys every yoke on my life. I decree that I am healed and Spirit-filled. Sickness and disease are now far from me. I overrule, disallow, and veto every diabolical sanction concerning my life!

Rejoice and shout right now! Shout, "It's over! My history does not dictate my destiny. I nullify every diabolical decision concerning my ministry. I take control over the airways, galaxies, systems, and atmosphere. I call on Micah, the archangel, to put his arms around my house. It's over! Satan, you have no power! You have no authority! In the name of Jesus!"

Chapter One
Your History Does Not Dictate Your Destiny

_____

_____

_____

_____

_____

_____

_____

_____

_____

_____

_____

_____

_____

Rising to a Higher Level

I am sensing a strong shift, especially as it relates to men. Now more than ever, I sense men rising to a higher level spiritually. This is what we have prayed for; this is what we have believed God for. We are seeing men that are hungry for the things of God. This has to do with reclaiming. If we are born again, if we are to reclaim the earth, then we need to first understand that the supernatural is the foundation for all things. There is some reclaiming we need to do as men of God. There is some reclaiming we have to do as it relates to our personal life. There is some reclaiming we need to do as it relates to our home life and as it relates to our bloodline.

When Christ came, He was called the last Adam. There was a first Adam, and he failed. Because of this, we lost our right to the tree of life. This is when the last Adam came which was Jesus Christ. The natural realm became predominate in human life when Adam and Eve fell (Refer to Genesis 3:7). They became self-conscious rather than God-conscious. After Adam and Eve became self-conscious, when the Lord came through the garden, all of a sudden, they covered themselves with fig leaves when before it didn't matter that they were naked because they were innocent. When you lose your innocence, things will shift and change on you.

Adam and Eve became sense-oriented instead of Spirit-led. Remember, God actually speaks to our spirit so our mind has to be renewed. Since Adam and Eve became sense-oriented, they became limited to information in their minds rather than revelation in their hearts. Before the fall, Adam and Eve operated at a completely differently level in every area. They were at a higher level of understanding in victory, joy, peace, prosperity, peace, and power. They experienced a higher level of knowledge called revelation knowledge. We need revelation. We need wisdom. We need revelation knowledge, and this is what the Word of God will do for you. Revelation is when God starts revealing things to you as a man of God, a woman of God, or a child of God.

Everything was extraordinary, and Adam and Eve were extraordinary. You and I are extraordinary. There is nothing about you and I that is ordinary. We are Christ-like.

When Jesus came to the earth, He came as the last Adam and demonstrated where Adam and Eve operated before the fall. Christ came preaching the Kingdom of God, the Kingdom that we live in when we are born again. When we are born again, the Kingdom comes with Word and with enough power to bring itself to pass in our lives. The Kingdom will produce more than enough for us. It always does.

There are two aspects of the Gospel. First, there is the Gospel of Jesus Christ, which is the Gospel that brings a person to salvation. Secondly, there is the Gospel of the Kingdom of God. This is the Gospel that unhooks a person from the world's system. This is the Gospel that tells a person that while you are thanking God every day for your job, know that your job is not your source, God is. You may show up for work every day on time and be the best employee they have but your job is not your source. Christ is your source. Philippians 4:19 (NKJV) says, *"and my God shall supply all your need according to His riches in glory by Christ Jesus."* Be careful, don't make your job Jesus.

The Gospel of the Kingdom of God is instructions in God's Word to depend on and to serve God, not this world. The Gospel of the Kingdom of God is the Gospel Jesus preached about and taught about. The Gospel of the Kingdom of God is a new order of living by faith. As a member of the body of Christ, we need a revelation of this Kingdom life. As men of God, we have to live this Kingdom life, and we have to breathe it. We need revelation.

We are talking about, *So Goes the Man, So Goes the Family.* Don't you know that there is more to this life? Don't you realize that you haven't seen anything yet? Does anybody beside me believe that according to 1 Corinthians 2:9-10 (NKJV), *"eye has not seen, nor ear heard, nor have entered into the heart of man the things which God has prepared for those who love Him. But God has revealed them to us through His Spirit."* I just think you are on the verge of something big, something major because your life right now is going to another level.

We are made to operate on the same supernatural level that Adam and Eve operated on before the fall. Adam could speak to something, and it was done. When we received Jesus, He brought us in on that level. It's like there was no fall. Why? Because He restored it! We were made to live in a Kingdom that produces more than enough for us. We can do more. We have not seen anything yet, and I believe it's going to begin with the men. The man is going to have to catch this thing. The man has got to be the one that says, *"... as for me and my house, we're going to serve the Lord"* (Joshua 24:15 NKJV).   The man has to be the one to man-up, get into the Word, and pray.   The man has to be the priest, prophet, and king of his home.   Shout, "I am rising to another level right now!"   To get there, we need revelation of the Kingdom of God.

Then God said, *"Let us make man in Our image, according to Our likeness; let them have dominion over the fish of the sea, over the birds of the air, over the cattle, over all the earth, and over every creeping thing that creeps upon the earth"* (Genesis 1:26 NKJV).

Walking in Dominion

God created us to function just like Him in the earth, just like His Son.   Say, "I receive that."   Now, if you receive that, there should be nothing hindering your life right now.   I didn't say there is nothing that won't come against you.   It's going to come against you, but you can't let that stop you.   You've got to be a faith walker.

God gave us dominion which means He gave us rule and lordship over all the earth.   He made us to govern and manage the earth and its resources in the very beginning.   Genesis 1:27 (NKJV) says, *"So God created man in His own image, in the image of God He created him; male and female he created them."* Humans didn't create God.   I don't even like using the word "created" by me.   I can't create anything. I can design things but God is the Creator.   The created (humans) will never be God.   We will never be El Shaddai, God Almighty.   Yet, God gave us authority and responsibility over the earth's resources.

Genesis 1:28 in the Amplified Bible says, *"And God blessed them and said to them, be fruitful and multiply, and fill the earth, and subdue it (using all its vast resources in the service of God and man) and have dominion over the fish of the sea, the birds of the air and over every living creature that moves upon the earth."* God placed vast resources in the earth such as water, animals, wood, and gold.   Then, He gave Adam and Eve dominion over everything that He put in the earth.   God told them to subdue it.   In other words, God is saying, "I'm not going to subdue the earth for you.   You will have to subdue the earth because it is under you."

Psalms 115:16 says, *"The heavens are the heavens of the Lord, but the earth He has given to the sons of men."* God intends for this earth to be ours.   We are supposed to rule it and subdue it.   However, we can't do anything without Him.   Adam and Eve discovered this when they sinned and became separated from Him.   When Adam and Eve sinned, they bowed their knee to Satan, and their sin separated them from God putting them under spiritual authority of God's enemy, the devil.

And you were dead in your trespasses and sins, in which you formerly walked according to the course of this world, according to the prince of the power of the air, of the spirit that is now working in the sons of disobedience. Among them we too all formerly lived in the lust of our flesh, indulging the desires of the flesh and of the mind, and were by nature children of wrath, even the rest. But God, being rich in mercy, because of His great love with which He loved us, even when we were dead in our transgressions, made us alive together with Christ by grace you have been saved, and raised us up with Him and seated us with Him in the heavenly places in Christ Jesus.

Ephesians 2:1-6

Everyone in the world was at one time in the category of disobedient people under the control of demon spirits. However, by the grace of Jesus Christ, God raised us up together with Christ and seated us sit together in heavenly places in Christ Jesus. 1 John 5:19 says, *"We know that we are of God, and that the whole world lies in the power of the evil one."* Everyone in the world who has not been born into the Kingdom of God is under the deception of Satan. Revelation 12:9 calls him, *"That old serpent called the devil and Satan, which deceives the whole world."* Satan deceived all of us at one time.

When Jesus died, He paid the price for every person's sin and gave each of us a way back to God. When He rose again, He defeated the devil in open combat and stripped him of all spiritual authority that he had over Adam. This means that the devil has no more authority over you, over me, over your household, over my household, over your life, or over my life.

In the second chapter of Hebrews, verses 14-15, it explains how Christ became a man to defeat the devil and to free us from the devil's death grip on our lives. In Revelation 1:18, Jesus said, *"And the living One; and I was dead, and behold, I am alive forever more and I have the keys of death and of Hades."* This means that the keys of hell and death are now in Jesus' hands and through Jesus, we can be free of Satan's spiritual authority, reconciled to God, and live under God's spiritual authority. We don't have to walk in fear of death and hell but walk in faith and in the confidence of everlasting life in Christ Jesus. The only keys that we should be concerned with are the keys of the Kingdom of God that Jesus gives us when we read His Word.

And I will give you the keys of the kingdom of heaven, and whatever you bind on earth shall be bound in heaven, and whatever you loose on earth shall be loosed in heaven.

Matthew 16:19

The Kingdom of God

Jesus has given us the keys to the Kingdom of Heaven. I believe the keys are the Word of God. As sons and daughters of God, we now have authority in his name to storm the gates of hell. We can speak things that are not as though they were and all of Heaven backs us up. In His name, we cast out devils. In His name, we can lay hands on the sick and they will recover (Mark 16:17-18). In His name, we can call in resources. It is in His name that we can speak to a mountain, and it will be moved according to Mark 11:23.

Jesus has legally restored us to God. When we operate in the authority of the name of Jesus, every resource in this earth becomes subject once again to the Kingdom of God. Every place we set our foot on becomes Holy ground, and Satan and the disobedient that are following his influence are defeated. Jesus has legally restored us to our Heavenly Father and given us His authority, the authority of His name. Furthermore, as children of His Kingdom, all the riches of God and heaven are ours. However, we have to know how the Kingdom of God operates in order to access what He has given us.

As we receive revelation of the Gospel of the Kingdom of God, we will rise to a higher level in every area of our lives. The standards of this world and its system are much below the standards of heaven. For example, in the economic system in the earth, when we invest money we expect to receive interest back. One hundred percent interest or doubling an investment would be a great return. In the Kingdom of God, we are able to bank on another level. We are able to sow a seed and receive 30, 60 or 100 fold. The spirit is the part of us that will receive revelation in the Kingdom. Proverbs 27:20 says, *"The spirit of man is the candle of the Lord, searching all the inward parts of the belly."*

God guides us through our spirit and not our mind.

Psalm 18:28 refers to the spirit as a candle: *"For thou will light my candle, and the Lord my God will enlighten my darkness."* God's revelation will bring light where there has been darkness in our lives. We were created to operate on a much higher plane than just head knowledge. We were made to live by revelation in our heart by the Lord lighting our candle (spirit) and enlightening our darkness (understanding). When we do, we can see what the world can't see, the Kingdom of God. If we don't have the knowledge of God, we cannot come out of the world's system and into the Kingdom.

Grace and peace be multiplied unto you thru the knowledge of God, and of Jesus our Lord, according as his divine power has given unto us all things that pertain unto life and godliness, thru the knowledge of him that has called us to glory and virtue; whereby are given unto us exceeding great and precious promises that by these you might be partakers of the divine nature.

2 Peter 1:2-4

The knowledge of God is revelation knowledge. It's not natural knowledge. It's through this knowledge that we obtain the great and precious promises of God's Kingdom. In Hosea 4:6 God says, *"My people are destroyed for a lack of knowledge."*

Real wealth doesn't come by education, it comes by revelation.

In the summer of 2008, an economic earthquake came, and it wasn't education that saved us. We need revelation on how to stand on the rock and how to receive our provision directly from Almighty God. This is why the Kingdom of God must be preached.

The Kingdom of God is God's way of doing things, and it comes with provision. Through His Kingdom, God has given us everything that we will ever need independent of what happens in the world. We are supposed to be restoring people to wholeness in the name of Jesus (Mark 16:18). We have something that will turn them in another direction and satisfy them so that they will never need to take another drug. We have the Holy Spirit.

Jesus asked his disciples, *"'Who do men say that I, the Son of Man, am?' Simon Peter said, 'You are the Christ, the Son of the living God.' Jesus said, 'Simon Bar-Jonah, for flesh and blood has not revealed this to you, but My Father who is in heaven. And I also say to you that you are Peter, and on this rock I will build My church, and the gates of Hades shall not prevail against it.'"* (Matthew 16:13-18 NKJV).

Simon was flaky, but Peter was a rock. Simon Peter went from being flaky to being solid because of what he could see. The reason the gates of hell could not prevail against Peter is because now, he could see the Kingdom. Peter had the light. He had the revelation. Notice that it was the Father who revealed who Jesus was.

Most believers don't have this revelation because their hearts are not set to depend on God. They are still locked into this world as their source. God says, "I don't want the world to be your source. I want to be your source. I want you to be locked into Me. You are under a new government with a new King who wants to take care of you."

Reflections

Chapter Two

Rising to a Higher Level

_____

_____

_____

_____

_____

_____

_____

_____

_____

_____

_____

_____

_____

Men need relationships. This is why men will hang around the barbershop long after we've gotten a haircut or even when we don't need one. Men want that type of fellowship that we can't necessarily get from our spouse. However, you cannot hang out with negative people and expect a positive life. It is impossible. As the man, it is your responsibility to meet negative people at the door, and let them know that they are not welcome. As the priest, prophet, and king of your home, you cannot allow any negative person to contaminate your family. So Goes the Man, So Goes the Family!

Let's put some Bible on it, and look at Matthew 5:43-48 (NIV):

You have heard it said, 'Love your neighbor and hate your enemy.' But I tell you, love your enemies and pray for those who persecute you, that you may be children of your Father in heaven. He causes his sun to rise on the evil and the good, and sends rain on the righteous and the unrighteous. If you love those who love you, what reward will you get? Are not even the tax collectors doing that? And if you greet only your own people, what are doing more than others? Do not even pagans do that? Be perfect, therefore, as you heavenly Father is perfect.

Jesus uses the words "pagans" or "tax collectors" in verses 47 and 50. Basically, Jesus is saying (paraphrased), *"If you just love people who love you back that even the street people and crooked people do that."* It doesn't mean that you shouldn't love people that you don't hang with. You can love people and still not hang with them. Prior to getting married, I had four very close friends. We were as close as David and Jonathan in the Bible, but we were not in Christ. These friends meant a lot to me, but I knew those relationships would not be good for my marriage. The reason is that people will change you before you change them.

Fellowship and Relationship

Then one of the scribes came, and having heard them reasoning together, perceiving that He had answered them well, asked Him, 'Which is the first commandment of all?' Jesus answered him, 'The first of all the commandments is: Hear O Israel, the Lord our God, the Lord is one. And you shall love the Lord your God with all your heart, with all your soul, with all your mind, and with all your strength. This is the first commandment. And the second, like it, is this: You shall love your neighbor as yourself. There is no other commandment greater than these.'

Mark 12:28-31 (NKJV)

They were asking Jesus to pick out the most important commandment from the Decalogue or the Ten Commandments. Jesus is saying that you have to love every single person in the world. Jesus is not saying that you have to hang out with everybody. Do you know how difficult that is? The truth is, we can't do it! It is He, through us, who gets it done.

Let me make this point: Even if it's the worst person in the world, you still have to love them. I'll bring it closer. You have to love all your exes, your enemies, your haters, and the people who pained you. You have to love them! One of the hardest things about being saved is loving people that can't stand you. You may see them some place, and you have to wave and speak to them in a cordial manner. The Bible says that you have to love everybody, but it does not say that you have to hang with everybody. All of us have been hurt before, but you cannot go to the next dimension until you forgive those who have wounded you. Forgiveness is for you. Not for the people who pained you. Forgiveness allows you to get back into your flow with God again.

Second Corinthians 6:14-16 (NIV) says, *"Do not be yoked together with unbelievers. For what do righteousness and wickedness have in common? Or what fellowship can light have with darkness? What harmony is there between Christ and Belial? Or what part has a believer with an unbeliever? And what agreement is there between the temple of God and idols? For we are the temple of the living God. And God has said: 'I will live with them and walk among them and I will be their God, and they will be my people.'"* This scripture is basic Christianity 101. It is nothing deep. Any believer that has a little Word in them knows that a Christian cannot hang out with sinners. Of course, we have to be involved with sinners because it is our responsibility to get them saved. That is an assignment. A relationship is much deeper. We are assigned to go make disciples of all men. Why do you think that people at work or in public keep running up to you telling you about their issues and asking for prayer? That's not a relationship. That's an assignment. You have to know the difference.

In 1 Corinthians 5:9-10 (NIV), Paul writes, *"I wrote you in my letter not to associate with sexually immoral people. Not meaning all the people of this world who are immoral, or the greedy and swindlers, or idolaters. In that case you would have to leave this world."* Let's talk about what Paul did not say in this passage because most people exegete that passage incorrectly. Paul did not say that Christians should not have any contact with unbelievers. You would have to leave this world to not be involved with sinners. Paul is saying that the people that you really need to avoid are those people who are in the church and are nasty. If you've ever noticed for the most part, street people still have respect for and honor God. It's the church that they don't like. The reason is because there are those among us who are bad examples – gossiping and speaking ill of God's anointed. Paul is saying to avoid those who are preaching, teaching, singing, and acting like they love God. Paul is referring to those who are pretending to be one thing but doing another – singing "Amazing Grace" on Sunday and Baby Face on Monday. Paul is saying, "I'm not saying to avoid people outside the church who do that because you would have to live on Mars to avoid fornicators and liars." You have to deal with people in order to get them saved.

When you study Christology, you will find that Jesus was always dealing with crazy people. Remember, when He dealt with the woman at the well? He dealt with Zacchaeus' crooked and lying self. He was always dealing with crazy people while on earth. You have to deal with people on your job in order to get them saved. Your job is the marketplace and the harvest field. It is your responsibility (assignment) to reach people for Jesus wherever your assignment may be not behind a microphone at church.

There is a difference between evangelism and relationship.

There is a difference between you dealing with someone because you're trying to get them saved and dealing with someone on an ongoing basis. You were created for fellowship and relationship. Genesis 1:27 (NKJV) says, *"So God created man in His own image, in the image of God He created him; male and female He created them."* You were made in God's image. God has a relationship even with himself – the Father, Son, and Holy Spirit. He's a relational God. The Lord God said, *"It is not good for the man to be alone. I will make a helper suitable for him"* (Genesis 2:18 NIV). When the Bible says, *"It is not good for man to be alone",* that's exactly what the scripture meant. It is not good for man to be alone. We were created for fellowship. God does not want us to be alone.

Do you know what prisons do to prisoners when they really want to drive them crazy? They put them in solitary confinement. In turn, some of those prisoners lose their minds because we were not created to be isolated for a long period of time.

Covenant Relationships

I've given you the foundation, but you may ask, "Who should I hang with?" Here's my first question: Whom do you hang with right now? Who do you talk to on a daily or consistent basis? Who do you text? Here's my second question: Why do you talk to them? What do you gain from this relationship or friendship? Is this relationship or friendship substantial, and does it increase you? How are you better off because of talking to them? Now, I did not ask you if it stimulates you. I asked you if it is substantial because everything that stimulates you is not substantial. I did not ask you if it was fun, because everything that is fun is not building you. I did not ask you if it was entertaining because people can be cursing on the phone and have you laughing. I didn't ask you if they make you laugh. People can do all of that, but is it building you spiritually?

In a God-ordained relationship or friendship, there should be commonality.

I know that you are aware that God did not send everyone who is in your life. So, you ask, "What do you mean by commonality, Bishop?" I'm glad you asked! Here is what I mean by commonality. Do you both love Jesus, and are you both fully committed to God's will, Word, and His way? I'm talking about your friends and not the person you married. I'm referring to your friends, your associates, your cousins, your mom, your brother, maybe your sister, or whoever you are talking to on a regular basis. Do you both love Jesus?

Most saints are nominal at best. The Bible says in James 2:19 (paraphrased), *"The devil believes and trembles. The devil himself believes that God is real and trembles at His name."* Let me break it down to you. Your best friend cannot be a sinner! "But Bishop, one day when I didn't have anybody she [he] was there for me. That's my girl [my boy]!" I believe she [he] was there for you, and I know that she's your girl [he's your boy], but your girl [your boy] is not saved! If they don't love Jesus, then what are you all going to talk about? I'm not trying to restrict you to talk about Jesus only. Sure, you can talk about sports, which I love. You can talk about politics and other things, but if you really love God like I do, you have to say His name if you keep talking. You can't have a friend that always asks you, "Why do you have to always bring up church?" Church is all I know! Praise is what I do! Everything that I see reminds me of God's goodness! If your best friend is not in church, then there's an issue with that unless you are trying to win them to Jesus.

Here's my third question: Did God place them in your life? Your relationship must be a covenant relationship.

After David had finished talking with Saul, Jonathan became one in spirit with David, and he loved him as himself.

1 Samuel 18:1 (NIV)

David and Jonathan were not homosexual lovers. In the Mediterranean culture, friendship meant something. In America, we cannot understand a covenant relationship because we drop our friends on a dime. Covenant means that I'm going to give you my heart; now, you give me yours. Covenant means I'll be there for you no matter what. In Mediterranean culture, friendship covenant was like a marriage covenant. The way you say, "I do" in marriage is the way you made friends in that culture. That's why David and Jonathan were so close. If God gives you one covenant friend, praise Him for that! Don't look for five or ten because that's too many. I have a lot of major preachers in my phone, but when I need someone to talk to, I don't look for big names. I call a covenant brother because we have things in common.

Here's my fourth question: Do you have the same marital status? I did not say that if you are married then you cannot have single friends, or if you are single, you can't have married friends. Let me be clear. If you are married and they are single, there are some things they are not going to understand and vice versa. How can they give you martial advice? I believe your covenant friend should have your same marital status.

Here's my next question: Do they challenge you beyond your limitations and expectations? Let's tie in what we've discussed so far. Do not hang with all dumb people so that you can feel smart. If you are the smartest person in the crowd, then you're in the wrong crowd. Don't tell me that it doesn't matter which church you go to because it does matter. You need a Word that will bless and challenge you all at the same time. You need a Word that tells you that you can keep yourself as a single individual. You need a Word that tells you that you can stay married and be happy in your marriage. You need a Word that tells you that your money can get better. You need a Word that will tell you that greater is coming!

I am careful with whom I talk to because words have power. You are giving whomever you talk to access to your soul, and they are imparting into you. Are they imparting negativity, or are they imparting Kingdom principles which tell you that you can do all things through Christ who strengthens you? If you are broke then don't have all broke friends. Get you one friend with money, and say things like, "I don't want any of your money. Show me how you're tithing and saving. Show me how to start a business. Teach me how to invest."

Finally, do they empower your prayer life? When you talk to them do they say, "Let's pray about that right now?" no matter what you bring up? *Who Are You Hanging With?* Someone has to stand on top of that pit, reach down, and say, "Let me speak into your life. Your marriage will survive. Your money is changing! Your house will not foreclose because my God will supply all of your needs, and I put my faith with your faith! If one can put a thousand to flight then two can put 10,000 to flight!" If you hang with all dumb, broke, and nasty people then you aren't coming out of that pit. They'll be loyal in the pit, but you won't get out.

Do you want to get up? I am not going to write about a defeated theology! The devil is a liar! Maybe you have been to hell and back, but you have decided that your latter shall be greater than your past? You should talk about where you are going and not where you have been. You have been hanging with negative people so long that you function comfortably in dysfunction. Do the people that you hang around complain? Do they have a vision? Don't let anyone kill your vision. Speak this right now: "Vision is on my life!"

Who do you talk to that makes you believe that you cannot win? Satan wants to attack your mind and the best way is through the people that you talk to. This is because one of the gates to the heart is the ear gate. All of your friends shouldn't be needy and parasitic. You need someone in your life who imparts into you. You must know the difference between a relationship and an assignment.

Chapter Three
Who Are You Hanging With?

_____

_____

_____

_____

_____

_____

_____

_____

_____

_____

_____

_____

_____

So Goes the Woman

Reflections by Pastor Anita F. Jackson

I am honored to be able to reflect on this book that has been written by my husband, Bishop Getties L. Jackson, Sr. Bishop has asked me to reflect on what I have read and how, as a woman of God, the chapters speak to me. I pray that you will take these principles and apply them to your life as well. Paul said in 1 Corinthians 11:1 (NKJV), "Imitate me, just as I also imitate Christ." I have no problem following Bishop as he follows Christ. So Goes the Man, So Goes the Family.

So Goes the Woman   **Chapter One**
Your History Does Not Dictate Your Destiny

As I reflected on the life of Josiah, one of the first things that stood out to me was how young Josiah was when he became king. Even in his youth, Josiah knew that he had to demolish those things from the past, the things that would hinder him from who God called him to be. In order for us to go forward, we need to meditate on 2 Corinthians 10:4-5 (NIV), *"The weapons we fight with are not the weapons of the world. On the contrary, they have divine power to demolish strongholds. We demolish arguments and every pretension that sets itself up against the knowledge of God, and we take captive every thought to make it obedient to Christ."* In my own life, I have had to pull down, cast down, and throw down the things that try to hinder me. I have had to stand firm on the Word of God. Remember, we are victorious over the devil through God. Keep your armor on (Ephesians 6:11). Walk in your purpose and your destiny!

So Goes the Woman # Chapter Two
Rising to a Higher Level

Joshua 24:15 (NKJV) says *"...as for me and my house, we're going to serve the Lord."* As I read that verse, all I could think about was my husband. Many, many times throughout the years, no matter what was going on, Bishop has always stood on this truth. I am so proud of him for being the priest, prophet, and king of our home. I have watched my husband, as he says, "man-up, get into the Word, and pray" for our family. I have watched him live this Kingdom life, and I have watched God take him to a higher level.

So Goes the Woman # Chapter Three
Who Are You Hanging With?

As a woman of God, I have had to be very alert at all times and pray for spiritual wisdom. God will always show you what is right or wrong. He will always show you who is for Jesus and who is not. God will put you with the right people if (and that is the key), if you will listen. Many times, the Spirit of the Lord will show you things, and you may choose to push pass it and think that you know better. As I think about covenant relationships, I think about John 15. Read it, study it, and meditate on it. You will understand truth about relationships and fellowship.

Part II

Walking in Purpose and Destiny

Chapter Four
God Wants You in Purpose

No one is satisfied until they are in purpose, Christian or non-Christian. If you are born again and you are not in purpose, then you are hard to live with. We all have been there. When you are not in purpose, things can be chaotic. You may be in purpose and right where God wants you. The Apostle Paul says, *"Now godliness with content is great gain"* (1 Timothy 6:6 NKJV). You have to understand that even though you are in purpose, your call is always evolving. Calls are always expanding, and there are calls within calls. God will not say anything else until you obey and follow preceding order. You have to obey what he has called you to do. Many of you haven't heard anything else because there are assignments He's called you to do, but you haven't carried those out yet. You are in disobedience. He is not going to give you another order until you as a man of God, women of God, or child of God obey the preceding order.

God said to Abraham, "Abraham, leave your country." Abraham asked, "Where am I going?" God replied, "I'll tell you that when you start walking." God said leave your father, mother, and all your kinfolks because they are messing you up. Abraham is known as the Father of the Faith. If Joseph had known about the pit and the prison, then he would have never made it to the palace.

What if God told you, "I'm taking you to the palace, but before you get there you are going to be thrown into a pit, lied on, and thrown into prison? If you make it through all of that, you will be second to the king." Let's make it practical. Let's say that God told you that he was going to send you to the White House and that you were going to be second in command to the President, but before you get there, you are going to be thrown into a pit and into prison. You would say, "Let me think about it, God." Everyone wants increase, everyone wants favor, but no one wants to go through anything. Before your promotion can come, you have to go through some things.

Most of us cannot handle the journey so God tells us enough just to get us started. Personally, I would not have been able to handle the journey if He had of told me everything that was going to happen on the journey. The Greek word *kalĕō* means, "to call by name, to invite, or to summon with a view to service". God doesn't just give us titles in the Kingdom to look good. Most of us get a title and then we get lazy. We don't deserve the title. I don't deserve to be called "Bishop". Without God, we can do nothing. We need more humility in the Kingdom. Luke 9:23 (NKJV) says, *"If anyone desires to come after Me, let him deny himself, and take up his cross daily, and follow Me."* The cross represents something had to be buried. What had to be buried? The flesh, that flesh that we got from our parents, the part that rebels within us.

Most men do not care. They are messing women up. They are blocking the blessing. Men are getting women pregnant and being a daddy but not a father. Men are concerned about everything else except the Kingdom of God. When you know better, you have to do better.

So God called, named, invited, or summoned believers to some special office or work of service. Every one of us. Whether you like it or not, if you are born again, you are a preacher. You don't like that, do you? The day you received Jesus that was the day you were called to proclaim the gospel of the Kingdom of God that Christ has risen. It is no longer about us. Paul says in Galatians 2:20 (NKJV), *"I have been crucified with Christ; it is no longer I who live, but Christ lives in me."* This body is nothing but a tent. One of these days, we are going to take off this body, and one day we are going to put on a body just like Jesus. If a man will catch it, he is holding up everything in the home. If a man will, instead of trying to make a living, start doing a Matthew 6:33 (NKJV), *"Seek first the kingdom of God and His righteousness, and all these things shall be added to you."* Philippians 4:19 (NKJV) says, *"And my God shall supply all your need according to His riches in glory by Christ Jesus:"* God has to supply for us. David said, *"God is not a man, that He should lie, nor the son of man, that He should repent"* (Numbers 23:19 NKJV). God will heal your body. If you will get in the Word, the Word will renew your mind. All of this will happen when you get in purpose. You have to get in purpose on purpose.

The call is from God, and the commission is wherever God places you. God may have called you to teach at a previous church, and He may have commissioned you to another. So, the call didn't change, but the commission did. You are called to help your church. *"Eye has not seen, nor ear heard . . ."* (1 Corinthians 2:9 NKJV). Watch, things will go to another level when you get involved in your church. You are important. The call is to salvation.

2 Peter 1:10 (NIV) says, *"Therefore my brothers and sisters, make every effort to confirm your calling and election. For if you do these things, you will never stumble."* You cannot get messed up when you know you have been called by God. The calling in 2 Peter 1:10 is "sal-viv-ic". It has to do with soteriology, the theology of how one becomes saved. Verse 10 reads like a service passage, but it is really a salvation passage. If you don't know Christ, He is calling you right now. He is wooing you right now. There is a place in your heart that was made for God. Without God, there is no peace, purpose, or passion. No man or woman, drugs or alcohol, pornography, lottery ticket, or anything else for that matter can fill your heart.

To the young people, don't be like the older ones. You had better start serving Him while you have the chance. There are always those who will complain. People who are not doing anything are always criticizing. People who are doing something know how hard it is.

The first thing the Holy Spirit does is woo you. He is drawing you. He is the third person in the Trinity. His name is the Holy Spirit. There are a lot of believers who have the Holy Spirit, but He doesn't have all of them. That is why some of you are still nasty, still cussing, and still going on to nasty websites. He will seal you until the Day of Redemption. He is going to shake you, and He is not going to let you sleep too late.

Have you been saved or baptized? Was it the Devil who told you to get up and come to the front of the church to be saved? So, you didn't have the Holy Spirit within you because you were not saved. You were between sin and salvation. What happened?

The Holy Spirit wooed you. He wasn't in you yet, but all of your life He was saying, "I not only want to woo you, but I want to come inside of you." So, the Holy Spirit wooed you and called you to salvation.

I get upset with some men. I want to kick some of them in the rear end. As a man, do you not know how many people are depending on you? *So Goes The Man, So Goes The Family.* Do you not know that your great grandmother prayed for you? Do you not know that greater is He that is in you than he that is in the world (Refer to 1 John 4:4)? Say, "I have to get in purpose."

Serving Faith

Secondly, there is a call to service. Some of you are involved in community activities, but you are not even involved in your own church. It starts at home. Romans 12:3 (NIV) says, *"For by the grace given to me I say to every one of you: Do not think of yourself more highly than you ought, but rather think of yourself with sober judgment, in accordance with the faith God has distributed to each of you."* You are called first to salvation but secondly, you are called to service. How would you feel at home if you are doing all of the work and no one is helping you? How would you feel, when people finished eating, they leave the plate on the table and wait for you to move it? How would you feel when the trash can is full and they are waiting on you to dump it? The same way it is in the church. Some of you have the gift of service that is why you cannot stand to see paper on the floor. You pick it up.

Paul is saying every believer has been given enough faith to start serving. I have crazy faith. I just believe that God can do anything but fail. On your way to destiny right now, you have serving faith.

If you don't hear God on big decisions then don't do anything! Big decisions like buying a house, getting married, quitting your job, who you should date, or any major decision in life. If God didn't tell you to do it, don't do it because these things can be catastrophic. Sometimes, you can make your move and regret it later. This is not the case when it comes to ministry. Ministry is the one area in life if you don't think you have anything, just start doing something. You should start by finding ministries in your church to assist in. For example, clean the church, help with the youth ministry, get involved in the singles' ministry, the women's ministry, the men's ministry, the ushers' ministry, become a greeter, join the praise team or choir, help with the parking ministry, etc. The point is get involved and connected in your church. A moving car is easy to turn, but a parked car is almost impossible to move.

God cannot speak to some because they are not doing anything. God wants you in purpose. If you haven't heard anything from God as it relates to ministry, do something. Everything you need is in your local church. However, if you're in a car (a ministry) that's moving and you're in the wrong car, God will say, "You know you can't sing. Get off the praise team, and help with the children." Get in a ministry that is closest to your gift. What is the difference between a talent and a gift? When people go to Drake or Beyoncé's concert, all they have is talent on the stage. A gift will remove burdens. Talents, you are born with. You get your spiritual gift at salvation. Maybe you dance well. That is a talent. You may ask, "Well Bishop, why do I enjoy it so much?" This means that you have the gift of exhortation.

You have been called to serve. The one thing every individual must do is hear God for themself. Your parents, spouse, prayer partner, or pastor can't do that for you. "Bishop, I want a husband or a wife." Forget that until you hear from God! Young ladies, learn how to keep yourself. I will show you how to get him to marry you. Put it on lock down - clang, clang! A man or woman might mess up your hearing even more. Everyone knows how much I love my wife, Pastor Anita. My kids definitely know it. My wife is my greatest investment, but I love my call and purpose more. I would be a terrible person if I were not in my call and purpose. I would mess up my wife. I would mess up our home. I would mess up the church that I pastor. I wouldn't like myself if I were not in purpose.

This is why God placed you on planet earth . . . for purpose. Don't let anybody come before that. You are not anything; you are not much without purpose. No one would want to be around me if I was not in purpose. It makes me easier to live with because a person with purpose has more peace. This is how frustrated people are; they are not in purpose. That is why people do not want to be around them. Some people may be terrible spouses because they are frustrated with themselves, and they take it out on their partner.

Submit to the Call

Thirdly, there is a call to an individual. I just don't believe that you should hook up with some "Co-Co Puff" that comes along. This is why I tell singles the more they can keep themselves pure, the more they can hear what God is calling them to do. I tell singles to keep themselves so they don't get in mess because shame will kick in because sin brings shame. Lust always has an expiration date, but the agape love will last for a lifetime. God will give you someone who will love you unconditionally. God will give you someone who will love you in spite of. So, it's all right to date as long as you don't do the stuff that brings shame with it. Learn to date when it is light. Something shifts when night comes.

First Corinthians Chapter 7 deals with the fact that some of us are called to singleness. How does God call? The Word of the Lord came to Jeremiah (Refer to Jeremiah 1:4) and to Moses (Refer to Exodus 3). These were cataclysmic calls. Paul's call knocked him down with lightning flashing and blinded him. God called, "Moses, Moses take off your shoes, you are standing on Holy ground." The bush is burning but not consumed. God called, "Abraham, get out of your country." You need to be under a covering. You are not a rebel or a renegade detached. Everything needs covering. My covering is Bishop Dale C. Bronner. You don't outgrow your covering because God has placed you under him. **Submit yourself.**

There are other ways that the Lord speaks. "But the Word of the Lord", this is the way God speaks to most people, internally. Another way God speaks to us is by a way of burden. Each week before I minister, I want to get the message that God placed inside of me to the congregation. Some of you, because you went through so much as a child, have this burden to help teenagers or children. You are an usher, you keep your house so clean and you are straightening up papers, because it burdens you that the house of God is not clean. That could be God saying to you that your calling is serving or the gift of helps.

Conviction is another way that God speaks. You may say, "I haven't heard God's voice but I feel led to help with the children, or serve as an usher, or work in the parking ministry, etc." Something ought to burn inside of you. The Word of the Lord is audible. I need you to understand that God can talk. Anachronistically, through our culture and the times that we live in, this culture is probably the least spiritual from previous generations.

Here's one, say, "Prophecy". Sometimes, God will give you a prophetic Word through someone else. It is similar to the Word of Knowledge. It should confirm something that you have been feeling. Stop thinking anachronistically and become more spiritual. Prophecy has not ceased. Sometimes, someone will walk up to me and ask, "Bishop, what has God said to you about me?" Be careful with that. Radical Pentecostalism has a Word for everybody. The point I am trying to make is there are times when the spirit is so high that I come out of the pulpit and say, "You, come here. God said you are hurting tonight, but your pain is for somebody else." Then, sometimes He's (Holy Spirit) not flowing like that, but whenever I give you a Word, I've got a Word! You may hear the Lord speak by hearing the Word of God preached or proclaimed. You may discover your call, gifts, and purpose by reading this book. Some are birthed into preaching by listening to their local pastor preach. Sometimes, God will confirm your call through the Word of God. These are all different ways of knowing the voice of God and your role in the Kingdom.

Also, there are visions (Refer to Acts 9:10). Visions seem to happen during the day, and dreams happen at night. When you sleep, God may come in a dream, but when you are awakened, God translates it. Have you ever been driving and you are almost home and thought, "How did I get home?" It's like an alternative state of consciousness, and your mind is on autopilot. God can take you into a vision where you are awake but you would call it a "day dream", and you caught yourself and realized you are in your living room, bedroom, or anywhere but not in that "day dream". For some, God revealed His call through a vision. If that's you, you saw yourself clearly doing what you've been called to do.

The Glory of the Lord

Now, refer to Genesis 22:11. Say, "Angel". Angels are real, and they are as real as a person sitting next to you. The problem is that you can't see them. They are here with you right now. All night, all day, angels are watching over you. Who do you think it was that kept that demon from going into your child's room and taking their breath away? God has placed an angel over your house who says the enemy cannot come in here because this is one of my children's houses. You have a personal angel who gets in the car with you, and you think you are driving, but God has the wheel. Do me a favor; thank God for the accident you didn't have. Angelology and you know many of them. Some of their names are Gabriel; Michael; and Rafael, the angel that heals.

He can make a way out of no way, and He can pay your house note while you are laid off. God is real. If He's not real, then what makes me feel so good? If He's not real, then what makes me cry when nobody is bothering me? You know there is something inside of you that keeps telling you that God is real! He can talk, and He can call you when everyone else has rejected you. God will come in your room and tell you, "I knew your end from the beginning." He'll say, "Your past does not dictate what I'm getting ready to do in your life." God says, "I'm calling you again." No matter what has happened in your past, heaven has stamped you and says that you are chosen to prosper. Wherever you may be right now, I want you to decree and declare this over your life:

God is calling me again. I believe that God is still alive and that He chose me to do something! I believe that the best is yet to come over my life! It's not over for me yet. Somebody is calling my name! There is a service in me and a call over my life. I'm getting ready to get busy for God in 2015, and this year will be greater than 2014! I'm getting my peace back! I got my joy back.

David encouraged himself in the Lord and danced until his clothes came off. Shout for your own future, your kid's future, and most of all, shout for destiny. Are you glad to be called by God? Are you glad that God knows your name? Are you glad that it's not over for you yet? Are you glad that your best days are ahead of you? Maybe you just heard from God. You don't want to be depressed, frustrated, or stuck in the same place. Somebody needs the glory more than they need the pillow on their bed. Say, "I need the glory! The glory of the Lord is on me!" The Bible says that the oil runs from Aaron's beard. If you get in line and apply the teachings in this book, you can't help but to be blessed! Before God gives you money, He's going to give you your mind, joy, and peace back. There's enough glory to restore your marriage and to fix your wounded spirit. Lift up your hands and say, "I receive the glory! I receive the glory more than money. I want God's glory in my life."

Chapter Four
God Wants You in Purpose

Chapter Five

We Have to Train Up Our Children

Let me be the first to tell you up front, that there are no guarantees, there are no formulas. There are many who bring their children up right in the Lord and the child goes in the other direction, the way of the world. We can only be responsible for what we are responsible for; that is to bring our children up in the fear and admonition of the Lord. Proverbs 22:6 tells us to *"Train up a child in the way he should go, even when he is old he will not depart from it."* The Old Testament promise literally says, "If you train up your child according to the child's personality, abilities, talent, and etc. when he is old, he will not depart from it." This is important, but it is not a promise that our children will never sin, never get in trouble, or will ever get saved. There is no promise or verse in the Bible that promises that. Again, you have to do your best to raise up your child in the nurture and admonition of the Lord.

I want you to understand that our children are free moral agents, and God does not have any grandchildren. There comes a day when they will have to choose. Your child has to choose to accept Christ for themselves. So, there are no guarantees. You can be a godly parent and have godly children, you can be a godly parent and have ungodly children, or you can be an ungodly parent and have godly children. You can go all the way back to the Garden of Eden, all the way back to Adam and Eve.

Remember, God was the perfect parent but Adam and Eve still messed up.

Sometimes, we look at our children and think that they are a reflection of our parenting. This is not always the truth. There are some parents who did a wonderful job. and their children just didn't turn out how they raised them. On the other hand, some of us know that our parents could have done a whole lot better, but God just graced us. There are no guaranteed formulas in particular for those that maybe single parents. Here is an important fact. It is not only quality time but it is quantity time spent with children that is important. The Bible does not talk much about single parents or children of single parents. The Bible talks about widows, orphans, and the fatherless.

A father of the fatherless, a defender of widows is God in His holy habitation.

Psalm 68:5

The Role of the Father

The text says, *"A father of the fatherless."* Who is God the Father in this context? He is the father for those who have no father. Now, for the man of the household, God says, "I don't have to be a father in your house if you are there in your place as the priest, prophet, and king of your household." He's God the Father but not in the context of the family. It is God's design that the man of the household be the father not just daddy because father means source. The only way a man is going to become the

- 70 -

priest, prophet, and king of the home is to become a man of the Word. You have to become a praying man. These things are vital. It was never God's intention to do what He has called us to do. God says, "I want to reflect who I am through you so that your children will see me in you." As Christians, we should reflect the heavenly Father. If you as the father live as you should as the priest, prophet, and king, then God doesn't have to show up on the scene. He's there through you. Now, I will tell you that it is hard work, but it is part of the calling.

God Loves Children

Children are special. Psalm 127:3a says, *"Behold, children are a gift of the Lord."* If you have a child, that is a gift. There are people praying to have a child and cannot have one. You are blessed if God has given you a child. Jesus said in Matthew 19:14 (NKJV), *"Let the little children come to Me, and do not forbid them. For such is the Kingdom of Heaven."* This is why when children ran up to Jesus, the disciples knew to leave them alone because Jesus said, *"Let the little children come to me."* Be careful how you treat children. Why? Because God loves children. Jesus said in Matthew 18:6 (NKJV), *"Whoever causes one of these little ones who believe in Me to sin, it would be better for him if a millstone were hung around his neck, and he were drowned in the depth of the sea."* Do not minimize what children can do in church or ministry. Do not minimize who they are. You do not know how God is going to use your children.

What should parents do since children are special to God? The Jews dedicated or gave their children back to the Lord. This was the case with Samuel. Samuel was taken to the temple and left under the care of Eli the Priest. Remember that Hannah, Samuel's mother, dedicated him to the Lord. Hannah said, "Lord, if you give me a baby, I'm going to give that baby right back to You." When God gives you anything, the first thing you should do is turn around and give it right back to Him. Have you given your children back to God? This is major. Raise your children to the best of your ability in Christ, pray for them, and bathe them in prayer. God will protect them and put a fence around them. They will be fine. At some point, you are going to have to use your faith for your children.

God granted this barren woman's request because she turned right back around and gave the child back to the Lord. That is what we should do. I hear parents saying, "I want my child to get a college education and live in a fine house." Yet, I don't hear many parents say, "I want my child to be saved." Have you taken the time to talk to your children one-on-one and asked them if they have received Jesus? It is never too late. If they are a teenager, you could ask them, "If you were standing before God and He asked you, 'Why should I let you into my Heaven?', what would you tell Him?"

Not only do we see dedication and consecration at an early age with Samuel, but we read it with Sampson in Judges 13:1-5. Why should our kids wait until they are old and gray to love and serve the Lord? That's the problem with most of us. Most of us waited until we are grown to love Him.

Raising Kingdom Children

I thank God for my grandmother and my mom because God knew I had an assignment to teach, preach, and pastor. You have no idea of how God may use your child as an agent of change. As parents, we must first dedicate ourselves to the Lord then dedicate our children to the Lord at birth. You must begin to speak into your children's lives. You are in a position where you can mold what your children believe. You can shape their minds because they are at the age where you can still influence them. The time to disciple your child and to put the fear of God in them is when they are small. The time to get your bluff in is when they are small. You may minimize that, but in the Bible, the father declares the blessing over the son (Refer to Genesis 49). The Bible says in Romans 4:17 (KJV), *"Calleth those things which be not as though they were."* Speak over your child until they become what you have spoken. I dare you to call your daughter, "Hey, Woman of God!" Call out to your son, "Hey, Man of God!" Speak into their lives and believe God for them. Here is an observation, the longer we wait to speak into the lives of our children, the less likely they are to receive Jesus as Lord and Savior.

Dr. Horananius Bonar compiled information from 253 converts (saved folks) with whom he was familiar. Dr. Bonar interviewed them, and below are his findings:

Out of 253 people that got saved:

- ♦ 138 of them got saved under 20 years old
- ♦ 85 of them got saved between the ages of 20 and 30

- ◆ 22 of them got saved between the ages of 30 and 40
- ◆ 4 of them got saved between the ages of 40 and 50
- ◆ 3 of them got saved between the ages of 50 and 60
- ◆ 1 of them got saved between the age of 60 and 70
- ◆ None of them got saved after the age of 70

Do you wish that you had met God earlier than what you did? After the age of 35, only one person in 50,000 receives Christ. After the age of 45, only one in 300,000 receives Christ. After the aged of 75, only one in 700,000 receives Christ. God's idea is for you to speak into your child's life now, because they were created to serve Him. Do not take for granted that your eight-year old son cannot be saved now. Start speaking into your child's life now! Do not spend more time reading and watching other stuff with your child than you do reading the Word of God. When you read a book to your child about Mickey Mouse or Dr. Seuss, make sure that you read Bible stories to them as well. Introduce them to Adam and Eve, Moses, and Esther now. Make sure that they are familiar with these real-life Bible characters. You are the one who determines what goes into your child's eye, ear, and mouth gate. They know too much about TV and not enough about the Word of God. We have to train up our children!

When our children get old enough and we didn't tell them about Christ, as parents, we will be held responsible. The Bible is a generational book: Abraham, Isaac, and Jacob. In Genesis 12:3 (NKJV), Abraham says, *"I will bless those who bless you and I will curse him who curses you."* What I do affects my children. We do not want to be doing negative stuff that will drop down on our babies. Proverbs 13:22 says, *"A good man leaves an inheritance to his children's children."* When we don't tell our children who God is, we risk our grandchildren not getting saved. So, what do all children need? They need confirmation. Listen to this:

- If a child lives in criticism, he learns to condemn.
- If a child lives in hostility, he learns to fight.
- If a child lives in fear, he learns to be apprehensive.
- If a child lives in pity, he learns to feel sorry for himself.
- If a child lives in jealousy, he learns to feel guilty.
- If a child lives in acceptance, he learns to love.
- If a child lives in approval, he learns to like himself.
- If a child lives in recognition, he learns to set goals.
- If a child lives in fairness, he learns what justice is.
- If a child lives in honesty, he learns what truth is.

You determine what your child will be in life. Every child needs confirmation from their parents. Every child needs discipline not punishment but discipline. Proverbs 13:24 (NKJV) says, *"He who spares his rod, hates his son, but he who loves him disciplines him promptly."* To confirm that scripture, Proverbs 19:18 says, *"Discipline your son while there is hope."* Deuteronomy 21:18-21 talks about a rebellious son who didn't obey his father and mother. The son wouldn't listen to his parents when they disciplined him. Deuteronomy 21:18-21 (NIV) says, *"His father and mother shall take hold of him and bring him to the elders at the gate of his town. They shall say to the elders, this son of ours is stubborn and rebellious. He will not obey us. He is a profligate and a* drunkard. Then, all the men of his town shall stone him to death. You must purge the evil from among you. All Israel will hear of it and be afraid."

Now, how did we get from that to time out? In my generation, if we showed out in public, our mothers went crazy because there weren't many cameras then. Men and women are different. So, when I disciplined my children, I knew how I wanted to discipline them. On the other hand, most moms put up with too much then when their children go too far, its bam! Children need correction. Proverbs 29:17 says, *"Correct your son and he will give you rest"* (comfort). Children need reproof because the Bible says, *"The rod and rebuke gives wisdom, but a child left to himself brings shame to his mother"* (Proverbs 29:15). A child needs discipline. Discipline comes from the root word "disciple". The aim of discipline is to build godly character that will cause a child's behavior to conform to the proper attitude, words, and actions. It is not the church's responsibility to discipline the child. It is the parent's responsibility to make disciples of their own children.

A child needs you to help them maintain good health by eating proper meals, exercising, and getting their proper rest. We must demonstrate love. Teach your children to accept responsibility. This is why you have so many grown men that don't want to get a job. That man's mother told him that he was Jesus all of his life. A grown man can find a place to work. Have you ever seen a spoiled grown man? He is quitting jobs and saying, "Man, they told me to pick up that box!" That's what UPS does, they pick up boxes! Teach your children to respect authority. I grew up in a generation where every respectable person in the neighborhood could whoop you: the principal, the teacher, a neighbor, etc. Teach your children to prepare for marriage and for a career. Most importantly, teach them to study the Word of God. The book of John is a great place to start.

Chapter Five
We Have to Train Up Our Children

_____

_____

_____

_____

_____

_____

_____

_____

_____

_____

_____

_____

_____

God Kept You Alive Because of Destiny Inside

Then they came to Jesus, and saw the one who had been demon-possessed and had the legion, sitting and clothed and in his right mind. And they were afraid.

Mark 5:15

Many people deal with the enemy trying to attack their mind. You may realize that if it weren't for the grace of God then you would have lost it. You may be borderline or perhaps you did lose it, and you're alive today only because of the grace of God. The grace of God is my favorite attribute of God. God's grace is Him giving us what we don't deserve. When something bad or catastrophic happens to you, you have three choices:

- ◆ **Choice 1 - You can let it define you.** Don't be defined by what happened or is happening to you. Failure is an event and not a person. You are not what you did! Never look for a man, woman, or things to fill a void that only God can fill.

- ◆ **Choice 2 - You can let it destroy you.** Don't let this be you. A sign of your breakout to your breakthrough is that you are tired. Remember Galatians 6:9 (KJV), *"And let us not be weary in well doing: for in due season we shall reap, if we faint not."* The operative word is "if".

- ◆ **Choice 3 - You can let it strengthen you.** Faith must be exercised. Whenever you go through storms in life, exercise your faith! Start making faith moves and placing your faith on things. Start saying things like, "Lord, according to your word…" Start quoting God's Word back to Him. Whenever you exercise your faith, you will get stronger in life. It's like physical exercise. If you keep doing it, your body will get stronger. God will allow storms to come into the lives of believers not to define us or to destroy us but to strengthen us!

In Mark Chapter 5, we are introduced to this man that has all the demons in him. He had so many demons in him that they called him Legion. Legion really means 6,000 Roman soldiers. Perhaps, there were so many demons in this man that we can't explain it all. In the text, Mark 5:1-2, "*They came to the other side of the sea, to the country of Gadarenes. And when He had come out of the boat, immediately there met Him out of the tombs a man with an unclean spirit.*" The night before, Jesus was at the bottom of the boat. The storm is crazy, and they panic. Jesus comes up to the top of the boat and says, "Peace be still." One version says, "Hush be quiet." Jesus goes back down to the bottom of the ship, and He goes back to sleep.

When the ship pulls back up to shore, we run back into another miracle. The text says that it was a dark and stormy night when the boat pulls up on shore. *"When Jesus got out of the boat, a man with an evil spirit came from the tombs to meet him"* (Mark 5:2). The man in the text has unclean spirits in him. He was unclean because of the demons. We know his geography.

The text tells us that *"He came out of the tombs."* However, we cannot deal with his geography until we first look at his biography.

When we meet the man in Mark Chapter 5, he was already crazy. I just believe that something jumped off in his life that drove him crazy. The Bible doesn't tell us anything about his mom or dad. It is silent about them. Yet, like him, there are some people in your life that were already crazy when you met them. All I'm saying is before you hate on them, why don't you ask the Holy Spirit what drove them crazy? I don't have his bio, but I believe something else happened. No one starts out that way, something happened.

Your History Doesn't Dictate Your Destiny

Then they came to Jesus, and saw the one who had been demon-possessed and had the legion, sitting and clothed and in his right mind. And they were afraid. And those who saw it told them how it happened to him who had been demon-possessed, and about the swine.

Mark 5:15-16 (NKJV)

The brother lives in a cemetery and is naked when he runs up to Jesus. He has chains on him, he's foaming at the mouth, and he lives in the graveyard. He was living among the dead! Be careful when you are comfortable in dead places and around dead people. The word "tomb" literally means *a place of remembrance.* This tells me that this man was stuck in the past. Something had jumped off in his life that he couldn't shake. The good news is that your history does not dictate your destiny! You must believe that you are here for a reason, and your purpose is greater than your challenges! The reason God kept you alive is because destiny is inside of you.

Not only did dead crazy people live in the graveyard but there were also cave-like apartments there. In Biblical times, if a person was really broke they would go live in a graveyard. This tells me that poverty is a type of demonic spirit. I don't believe that poverty is the will of God for your life. In Mark 5:3-4, it states that no one could contain him not even with chains. In the Greek, "damazo" means to tame a wild animal. Demons have power so don't let them in your life. That's why the Apostle Paul tells us to give no room to the devil.

Remember that period in your life when no one could control you? Do you remember that period in your life when you wouldn't listen to anyone, and all you dealt with were crazy people? No one could tell you anything. It was the period in your life when people with a strong anointing made you uncomfortable. You were in the wrong and knew it, but you weren't ready to stop. That was the period that you were crazy. Here's why you couldn't stop. The devil had his claws in you, and he could not release those claws until God said, "Let him go!"

There are just some things in our life that we can't mess with. Every spiritually developed believer knows that there is one sin that they cannot touch because they would go crazy and get off track. Paul put it this way in 1 John 5:15, *"There is sin that leads to death."* When you are wrong and you know that you are wrong, you don't even want to be around light. John 3:19 reads, *"This is the verdict: Light has come into the world, but people loved darkness instead of light because their deeds were evil."*

The text (Mark 5:4-5) does not say that others were cutting the man, but he was cutting himself. God has a plan for you, but most of the issues you are dealing with are ones that you cut yourself! Let me free you. Your spouse is going to cut you sometimes (not literally, but figuratively), and if you raise up a child in the Lord, they will grow up and may cut you as well. They may break your heart. Your job will cut you, and your family will cut you. Make up in your mind that others may cut you, but you're not going to cut yourself anymore! You have to pay your tithes, seek first the Kingdom, and not give the devil any room in your life. Wherever you attend church, you have to say, "I am going to pay my tithes." If you're married, you have to stay faithful to your spouse and not creep around on them. If you're single, you have to keep your life clean.

Forgetting the Former Things

There are three things you have to do to get to the next level and to your destiny. First, you have to repent. Confess your sins to God. Secondly, you have to reconcile. First, be reconciled to God then to others. Remember, forgiveness is for us not for them. Use wisdom when deciding which relationships to reconcile. Finally, you have to take responsibility. Stop blaming it on others. Say these words, "For all the wrong in my life, I repent, and I'm not going back. I need to reconcile and stop playing the blame game. I have to take responsibility to change my own life."

Have you learned your lesson? Philippians 3:13-14 is for those of you who keep going back to the people who cut you, ungodly relationships, the wrong crowd, back to the club, sneaking and creeping, or fornicating. You have to learn to stop it! One year from today, you can be better than you are right now if you take these principles and apply them to your life. If God raises dead folks, then He can resurrect your life!

In the text, the man did cut himself, but in Mark 5:6 it says, *"He saw Jesus."* If it wasn't for Jesus and for that name, where would we be? It's at the name of Jesus that every knee must bow and every tongue must confess that Jesus Christ is Lord to the glory of God the Father! We are changed because of Jesus. *"Therefore if any man be in Christ, he is a new creation: old things are passed away; behold, all things are become new"* (2 Corinthians 5:17 KJV). Praise God right now for every mountain and for every valley!

At the name of Jesus, demons have to tremble. Mark 5:6 says, *"Seeing Jesus from a distance; he ran up and bowed down before Him."* Now, we just discovered that this man was crazy, and demons had taken him over. So, it wasn't him that bowed but the demons that bowed to Jesus. The Bible does not say they worshipped Him as you know worship. Instead, the demons bowed to acknowledge. They bowed to acknowledge Jesus' deity. The fact that He is the hypostatic union, the homooúsios and the homoausios, fully man yet, fully God.

Demons understand that whenever God walks up, they have to acknowledge and bow down. This goes for whomever or whatever has been holding you hostage! They have to bow down today. Some of you are bound by alcohol, drugs, or even pornography, but I speak to the Holy Spirit that lives on the inside of you and command those spirits to bow and let you go!

The Son of God

You cannot believe in angels and not believe in demons. There is a branch of systematic theology called demonology. The systematic theology is Pneumatology, Eschatology, Christology, and Demonology. Here are three things about demons.

1. Demons believe that there is one God, and they tremble according to James 2:19.
2. They have nothing to do with Jesus. They are opposed to the clean spirit of Jesus. Evil spirits are diametrically opposed to Jesus, His purity, and His holiness. Demons are diametrically opposed to the light of Jesus. Some people will hate on you because of the light of Christ that is on you.
3. The Son of God has come to destroy the works of the devil according to 1 John 3:8b. Every demon that has raised itself against you has no power over your life.

I break every curse off of you in the name of Jesus. No witch can curse you, no sorcerer can hex you, and no family member can drive you crazy. No root worker can put a spell on you because you have the Holy Spirit inside of you. Everything that you thought that you couldn't get over, I speak to the Holy Spirit inside of you right now. You don't have to wait until the battle is over. You can open up your mouth and shout now! If your child is dealing with homosexuality, lesbianism, depression, or mental illness, I call it gone right now in the name of Jesus! I call your brother saved! I call your sister saved! I call your children healed! I call your sanity back in the name of Jesus. Be healed! Be delivered! Be set free! Make this declaration right now:

No weapon formed against me shall be able to prosper! He who has begun this good work in me shall perform it until the day of Jesus Christ. I'm the head and not the tail. I am blessed in the city.

When the demons saw Jesus in Mark 5:7, they said, *"What have I to do with you, Jesus, Son of the Most High God?"* In other words, "Jesus, why do you have to show up right now?" Jesus interrupted the devil's plan for your life because your set time for God's favor will not be interrupted! What the devil meant for evil, God meant it for good.

One theologian said that Jesus got right up in the man's face and said, "Who are you?" The man responded, "That's just the problem, I don't know who I am." The Bible says that Jesus cast the demons out of the man, and He cast them into the swine because the demons needed some place to dwell. Mark 5:15 reads that they saw the one who had been demon possessed and had the Legion sitting and clothed in his right mind, and they were afraid. The Bible says, "clothed". One version says that he screamed and howled all night. This was a crazy brother, but when Jesus got a hold of him, the same man that used to be crazy running around howling and cutting himself with stones was now calmly sitting with his legs crossed and may I say, "chillen like a villain". The Bible says, *"He who had been crazy."*

Chapter Six
God Kept You Alive Because of Destiny Inside

_____

_____

_____

_____

_____

_____

_____

_____

_____

_____

_____

_____

_____

_____

So Goes the Woman

Reflections by Pastor Anita F. Jackson

So Goes the Woman **Chapter Four**
God Wants You in Purpose

When I am walking in my purpose, things turn out so much better. Luke 9:23 is one of my life verses. Jesus says to all, *"If any man will come after me, let him deny himself, and take up his cross daily, and follow me"* (KJV). Two of the key words in this verse are the words "deny" and "daily". When I deny myself daily, I can answer the call to the teachings of Jesus because I am doing a Matthew 6:33, *"seek[ing] first the Kingdom"*. There is so much richness in this chapter, and it is spot on. The Holy Spirit will draw you to Him, if you will let Him.

For me, one of my purposes is to serve. I love to serve. Jesus came to serve. Mark 10:45 (NIV) says, *"For even the Son of Man did not come to be served, but to serve, and to give his life as a ransom for many."* I have kept that perspective throughout ministry, but in order for me to learn how to serve, I had to use the "three D" approach: Deny, Disciple, and Disciplined. When I deny myself daily because I am a disciple of Christ, I will and I can become disciplined to obey the Word of God.

So Goes the Woman **Chapter Five**
We Have to Train Up Our Children

I have always had to remind myself that our three children belong to God. I can say that we raised our children in the Lord. When they got older, that is when the true test came. I want to encourage parents, especially mothers that God is **NEVER** out of control. Your children might get out of control, but do not give up on them. Keep praying for them. Remember, nothing happens in life without the full knowledge of God. Also, remember that nothing is too great or too small for God to handle. I know that to be true in my life.

So Goes the Woman   **Chapter Six**

God Kept You Alive Because of Destiny Inside

I thank God for His grace. God knew me before I knew myself. God has placed a purpose, plan, and destiny inside of each one of us. On page 79, Bishop stated that many people deal with the enemy trying to attack their mind. I am one of those people. When I read this, it made me think about things I went through and how the devil attacked my mind. Bishop also stated that we have choices in how we handle these attacks. Scripture tells us that we have choices. Deuteronomy 30:19 (NKJV) says *"... I have set before you life and death, blessing and cursing; therefore choose life, that both you and your descendants may live."* I chose life. I chose to let the difficult times strengthen me rather than define or destroy me. When I go through the storms in life, I exercise my faith through the Word of God. Keep on your armor (Ephesians 6:11).

Part III

Staying Alive

Chapter Seven
The Fever is Broken

Now He arose from the synagogues and entered Simon's house. But Simon's wife mother was sick with a high fever, and they made request of Him concerning her. So He stood over her and rebuked the fever, and it left her. And immediately she arose and served them.

Luke 4:38-39 (NIV)

This world is permeated with evil, through and through. There are commercials that they show now that you did not see 25 years ago. People are afraid. This nation shifted; it has not been the same since 911. This is why it is important as believers that we put on the whole armor of God and be built up in the Holy Ghost. Yet, in the midst of fear, crime, and an evil world, the Word of God is still Good News. It is the only Good News. The Word of God makes it clear that Jesus has power over fear and power over evil. This is why we have to have scripture within us, knowing it verbatim and being able to meditate on it. When things hit you, be able to bring the scripture to your mind and speak the Word. It is very important that you mediate on the Word of God. John 10:10 says, *"The thief comes to steal, kill and to destroy. I have come that they may have life and have it more abundantly."* Are you living the abundant life? We are called to live the abundant life. You and I as born again believers are called to live the abundant life not mediocre. We are called to live in the pĕrissŏtĕrŏn in the

Greek, the overflow. This is the kind of life that you and I should be living. Christ said, *"I have come that [you] may have life and have it more abundantly."*

After Jesus had fasted and prayed for 40 days in the wilderness, He began his public ministry. Jesus taught in the synagogues in Nazareth and Capernaum. One day, Jesus went to Simon Peter's house. Dr. Luke noted that Peter's mother-in-law had a high fever. There was no Tylenol or aspirin to give her so Peter asked Jesus to come into his home to minister to her at sundown, when the Sabbath healing was permissible. You have to remember that they were still operating under the Law. That is why many of times that would try to trap Jesus and He would say, "I did not come to do away with the Law, the Law is actually fulfilled in me. I am the Law; I am more than the Law. I have come to give you some things that the Law cannot give you." We have to remember that although Jesus is always nearby, He must be invited into our homes to minister to us.

This is why our homes are chaotic because we have not invited Jesus, the great physician into our homes. We have not invited Jesus to be number one in our lives. We are not doing a Matthew 6:33 (KJV), *"But seek ye first the kingdom of God, and his righteousness; and all these things shall be added unto you."* It takes a father, he has to be the one, to invite Jesus into the home. So Goes the Man, So Goes the Family. Don't get this thing twisted. You have to invite Him in. How do I invite Him in? You have to be a praying man not a complaining man. You have to be a Word man and not a gossiping man. You have to be a man full of God's Spirit and not jump from the world. Are you getting this?

You have to be a man with the whole armor of God. You think you can't. I can't either but I can do all things through Christ. That's the whole key. Without Him, we can't do anything, but through Him, we can do all things. So, we have to invite Him in. Everyday, we have to invite Him in. Every moment, every hour, and throughout the day. As men, one of the best things we can do is gather our family together at home and say, "Lord Jesus, you are welcome back into our home again. Live Here. Abide Here." See if God is not there in your home, the thief is there. So God is not going to break in, you have to invite Him in.

Peter knew that if Jesus had the ability to rebuke a storm, the wind and the waves obeyed Him, surely, He had the ability to rebuke a fever. Jesus spoke to the wind and the storm and said, "Shhh!" He was really telling the disciples, "Ya'll settle down. I got this." You're not going to catch God off guard. I do not care what you are going through right now in life, it is not too big for God. Are you getting this? I don't care what you're facing right now, He's more than enough. I don't care what you're going through right now. I don't care how far to the bottom you have been I know what God can do. He'll take you down to bring you up. When you get up, you'll never get in your flesh again because you'll say, "If it hadn't been for the Lord that was on my side." He is making you to be more like Christ in the storm. When you go though things in life, you have to know that all things work together for the good. You have to trust Him all the way through it. When you go through things in life, you have to learn to trust Him no matter what it looks like. You have to tithe off your unemployment check. If all you get is $20, you have to give Him at least $2. Little becomes much when you put it in the Master's hand.

He is God all by Himself, and I believe He is going to settle some stuff. I believe He is speaking to some stuff right now. I believe He is putting marriages back together again. I believe He is telling singles, "You have to wait on me, now because lust has a termination date. I'm going to send you a Boaz, and when your Boaz comes, he is going to walk in the house with an agape love. He is going to love you when you are unlovable. He is going to love you when rollers won't stay in your hair." He is that kind of God. Give God some praise. Always keep a praise in you. Always train your spirit to praise God. Don't ever get so high and mighty and say it doesn't take all of that. You have to learn to praise Him because the God of the valley is also the God of the mountain. If you can praise Him, that is why David said in Psalm 23 (KJV):

The Lord is my shepherd; I shall not want. He maketh me to lie down in green pastures: he leadeth me besides the still waters. He restoreth my soul: he leadeth me in the paths of righteousness for his name's sake. Yea, though I walk through the valley of the shadow of death, I will fear no evil: for thou art with me; thy rod and thy staff they comfort me. Thou preparest a table before me in the presence of mine enemies: thou anointest my head with oil; my cup runneth over. Surely goodness and mercy shall follow me all the days of my life; and I will dwell in the house of the Lord for ever.

Give God a Davidic praise. Shout, "Glory, Glory!" Shout, "Hallelujah." You have to learn how to praise and worship God. You will start out in praise but it ought to end up in worship. You'll end up saying, "There's no one like Him."

When God breaks the fever in your life, that fever can represent a lot of things, it can represent generational curses, it can represent lack, that fever can represent anger, that fever can represent malice, that fever can represent lust, that fever can represent that you are in different towards the things of God, but whatever that fever is symbolic of in your life, that fever can be pornography, it can be an unforgiving spirit. The best way to get free in life is to forgive everybody that ever dogged you out in life. God breaks this fever then we go through something else. Let's say someone dogged us out then we're walking around with an unforgiving spirit that represents a fever. Whom the Son sets free, he is free indeed.

As soon as Jesus spoke the Word and rebuked the fever, the fever left. Some are trying to comprehend it with their mind. Our minds are too small to comprehend it. How do we comprehend it? By faith. Isaiah 55:8-9 (KJV) says, *"For my thoughts are not your thoughts, neither are your ways my ways, saidth the Lord. For as the heavens are higher than the earth, so are my ways higher than your ways, and my thoughts than your thoughts."* The same power that is in Jesus is in you. There's a you inside of you that you've never met. There's a you inside of you that He created to have dominion. That means take dominion. That means dominate. That means there should be nothing that is hindering your life right now. Here is the common thread that I am seeing. I see it more in men than I do women. When you see it in women, it is because the man does not know who he is. The man does not have clarity of his assignment. Don't become an old man in life or an old woman in life then decide this Word was true. You can get it now. We are going to have eternal life in heaven, but I believe we serve a God who wants us to have a slice of the pie right here on earth. The Bible tells us if an evil father knows how to give good gifts to his children how much more will our heavenly Father want to give to us (Refer to Matthew 7:11). What an oxymoron; an evil father and a Heavenly Father. God said there are no good things that He is going to withhold from them that walk uprightly (Refer Psalm 84:11). The other side of it is this, in Proverbs 28:13 (NKJV), the writer says, *"he who covers his sins will not prosper."*

Come on men. We have got to learn to put our big boy pants on. You may ask, "Bishop, everyday are you victorious?" Not in the natural but in the spiritual I am. There are days that I cry. There are days that I get knocked down. There are days that I get discouraged but I know where my help comes from. That's the difference. I understand the concept of Galatians 6:9 (KJV), *"And let us not [become] weary in well doing: for in due season we shall reap, if we faint not."* The problem with most saints is that they quit on God. Here is a sign you are about to walk in something big, something huge. Here's the sign, you've gotten tired. You are ready to throw your hands up. That's what God wants you to do is to throw your hands up and cry out to Him, "God, I can't do this." Exactly! Start speaking God's Word back to Him. Start quoting His Word back to Him. As we read further in the gospels, sometimes, Jesus laid hands on a sick person to do something unusual such as bathe in a river to be cured of leprosy or put mud on their eyes to receive their sight. No matter how Jesus chose to do it, the results were the same, complete healing. Say, "I am completely healed." I believe that. Say, "I am completely healed in my spirit, soul, and body."

Rebuke the Fever

Jesus has given us the same mandate and authority to rebuke in His name. Does your family ever see you praying as a man? I didn't say work. We're going to always work. That's the first thing that God gave Adam was a job. God told Adam to name these animals. I'm talking about getting in his presence. I am not trying to beat you up but to pick you up. We are on the same team. How long did you pray this morning or did you pray? You may say, "Bishop, I was tired." I was too. I work 7 days a week; have for years. See, it will work if you work it, but you can't be lazy. Are you getting this?

Sometimes, the fever is our family and it manifests it self through domestic violence. We watched daddy hit momma. We sit there as a son or daughter and the son is thinking, "Oh, that's how I am suppose to treat my wife when I get married years later." No, it's not! God took your wife from your ribs which is the closet part to your heart. Your wife is to be loved. She is to be cherished. Are you getting this? It's not that you don't love your family and friends, it's just that you have not allowed God to deal with your fever. Some of our family, friends, and relationships need healing from fever dysfunction or mental disease. You have to allow God to deal with your fever. So, when your temperature rises, you lift your hand or tongue to strike your loved ones. That is wrong. So Goes the Man, So Goes the Family. You cannot say just anything to your wife, children, and family. You cannot! Are you getting this? You cannot! You have to learn to let the words of your mouth and the meditation of your heart be acceptable unto God. You cannot just go back there and hit a wall. That's a fever that you got! You start cussing at your loved one. That's a fever that you got! This kind of fever can be healed only by the power and presence of Christ. So Goes the Man, So Goes the Family.

Let me talk to the men for a moment. As a little boy, I studied my dad. I studied my parents. While they were alive, I was a student of theirs. I knew my dad's strengthens. I knew my dad's weaknesses. I knew that it was only by the grace of God that I never got bitter. Make your big point, Bishop. As a man, you have to know what's in your bloodline. If your father loved women, you can't play with that. That will be your kryptonite. That's what will take you out. You cannot play with that. If your father liked to sneak around, you cannot play with that. It is not cute. You can choose to do it but only God is going to choose the consequence. If your father liked to drink, you can't mess with alcohol period. You shouldn't anyway but I am talking about period. It is so true that the only thing that is going to keep the apple from falling close to the tree is Christ. He will catch that apple, recreate that apple, and call you a new creature in Christ. Second Corinthians 5:17 (KJV) says, *"Therefore if any man be in Christ, he is a new creature: old things are passed away; behold, all things are become new."* You can do this Christ thing, here is the thing, you've got to want it. Every morning, I wake up and say, "I decide to do this Kingdom thing today. I decide to live for Christ today."

As a believer, we are the hands and feet of Jesus. He has called us to bring about healing and reconciliation. You cannot reconcile with everyone, but there shouldn't be anybody in your life that you are mad at. You have to make up your mind. Forgiveness is not for the other person but for you. Your healing will only come when you start forgiving people. Some people think that they are the only ones who have been dogged out. Everyone has been dogged out. Why? Because Adam ate the forbidden fruit.

Do you call yourself blessed in the city and blessed in the field? Are you the head and not the tail? By faith, are you out of debt and all of your needs met? Are you living in the place called "More Than Enough"? Are you in the place called "Overflow"? None of that will come until you start forgiving people. The reason I love that is because when people touch God's property, they mess up. It is a dangerous thing to put your mouth on God's property. Isaiah 54:17 (NKJV) says, *"No weapon formed against you shall prosper, and every tongue which rises against you in judgment you shall condemn."* One prophet went on to say in 1 Chronicles 16:22 (KJV), *"Touch not mine anointed. . ."* I've watched people over the years, dog people out, dog people out, and dog people out. I've watched God when the chickens come home to roost. What goes around comes back around. You cannot dog people out and think that you're not going to reap what you have sown. Christ is concerned about all of us and desires to heal us from our fever. He has called us to rebuke the fever in our family, friends, and relationships.

The story was told when Jesus returned to heaven after His resurrection. Gabriel greeted Him at the pearly gates. Gabriel asked Him, "Lord, do you have any other plans besides the great commission? What if it fails Lord?" Jesus replied, "No, I instructed Peter, James, John, and about 500 others, but to answer your question, no, I don't have any other plans."

I'm involved in a local church family. I'm a husband, a father to three grown children, a grandfather to two grandsons, and the son of the late Mr. & Mrs. Bobby Lee Jackson. I am also apart of the human family. The fever is rampant in our human family. Every 92 seconds, an African American child is born into poverty. Sixty-five percent (65%) of all African American families are headed by females. There's nothing wrong with mom, but this reveals the high fever that caused many of our fathers to be irresponsible. Some of them just don't care. They get a girl pregnant, mess her life up, marry her, and then dog her out like she's trash. Just irresponsible. Many of our men seem to have no problem of dropping a seed and then not caring about the results. I do not care how many children you have, take care of them. That is your seed. Don't make your children grow up hating you. If we're not careful, we'll pass this same fever on to our children.

Our nation has a high fever. The Iraq, North Korea, and United Nations conflict cannot be ignored. What should we do? We must seek the One who can rebuke the fever in our nation. We must call upon God while He can be found. God says in 2 Chronicles 7:14, *"If my people who are called by my name would humble themselves and pray and seek my face and turn from their wicked ways. I will forgive their sin and heal their land."* The world is not the problem; it is the people of God. God says in 1 Peter 4:17 (NKJV), *"judgment [will] begin at the house of God."* God is not going to start in the club, He is not going to start in the world, but He is going to start with us – the church. That shakes me in my boots to know that I have to be accountable as a husband, a father, a senior pastor, a friend, an uncle, a spiritual father, a brother, and a son-in law. That is too much! That's a lot knowing that one day it is going to be like yesterday we were in church.

We are talking about the One who has always been. We are talking about the Great I Am, the Alpha and Omega, the Beginning and the End, the Bright and Morning Star, the Great Physician, the Prince of Peace, El Shaddai, Jehovah Jireh, and Jehovah Shalom. That in itself should stop you from being nasty. You may ask, "Bishop, believers are nasty?" Yes, read 1 and 2 Corinthians. Paul was talking to the church. They were nasty. There are still a bunch of nasty believers today. One of the things that I discovered about the nasty believers is that they don't fear God. The difference is that those believers who are not nasty have the same thoughts but we have to cast them down.

In Jeremiah 29:11, God says, *"For I know the thoughts I think toward you, says the Lord, thoughts of peace and not of evil to give you a future and a hope."* God is working that thing out in your life right now, and you don't even know it. God has got that thing worked out. You may be saying, "Bishop, I don't know." Keep walking by faith. You may be saying, "Bishop, I don't know if He . . ." Keep believing He is going to do it. There is a difference between being positive and walking by faith. Faith is based upon the Word of God. Being positive is that Myers-Briggs stuff. I am talking about believing the Word of God for anything.

We should celebrate the fact that Christ can now break the fever. Christ came, and He tabernacled (pitched his tent) among us. Christ came, lived, died and rose again. Christ has the divine ability to break the fever in every family. He has given us the mandate to break the fever in His name. After Jesus rebuked the fever, the scripture says that Peter's mother-in-law got up from her sick bed and served them. She got up from her sick bed and said, "How can I help you?" She was so thankful to be well that she began to minister to those who had brought her healing.

The Power of Deliverance

We should never forget the preacher who turned us away from sin or our mother and father who loved us when we didn't love ourselves. We should never forget the church that reminded us that even in the midst of life's problems, God is still in control. We have a duty as the delivered. God brought us out to function as a part of the delivered community. Personally, I am so thankful to be apart of the delivered community. When I could not walk spiritually, God helped me step by step. When I was spiritually blind and could not see, God gave me sight. When I could not hear spiritually, God gave me the ability to listen to Him.

We all have the responsibility to reach behind us and pull up our family members who don't know how to get up on their own. Because we have been delivered, we have the obligation to reach out and fight the fever in others. We need to provide counseling in the church to break the fever of depression, unforgiveness, generational curses, mental disease, and family dysfunction. Some people may say, "I'm too busy to serve, I don't have time." You can reduce the fever with your checkbook. God can use compassion and money to open doors. What ministries are you committed to supporting? Is your church listed in your will? Are you going to leave something that will live from generation to generation to help break the fever as it manifests itself?

Jesus has called us to spread joy. Wherever we see depression or loneliness, we should spread joy. God has not called us to just shout in the church but to spread joy. Just as Simon Peter's mother-in-law served after she was healed and delivered, we too have an obligation to get up and serve. Some of us need to get up from selfishness and being self-absorbed. We need to get up from being lazy, and let Christ take our hands, our hearts, our mind, and our soul.

I have one thing to say over your life. Whatever your fever is symbolic of it is broken. Say, "I receive it in the name of Jesus." Here is the good news. It is not going to touch your children. There may have been some medical things that got in your bloodline, and you are afraid that it is going to hit you. Raise your hands right now, and thank God that it will not come nigh you. I do not care what that sickness is, it will not come near your children or your grandchildren. Here is the picture. The Holy Ghost is pulling it up by the roots. When you pull something up by the roots, it cannot come back in there any more. You had better thank the Holy Spirit that He is pulling it up by the roots right now.

He is going to take it to the land field and put it on one of those big mounds so it will dry out, die, and rot. Give God praise right now.

Chapter Seven
The Fever is Broken

Chapter Eight
Three Levels of Relationships

There are three levels of relationships that every believer ought to be involved in to keep reproducing. You don't just get saved and then do not relate to anybody. There has to be some accountability.

I love everybody, and as believers, we should too. But it's not the will of God, God's perfect will, for us to hang out with everybody. You want to be in God's perfect will. There is a major difference between His perfect will and His permissive will. There are some things that God will allow to happen, but it was not His perfect will.

There is a difference between evangelism and relationships. Don't get them mixed up. Some people are your assignment and that is all. You are not supposed to be going to the movies or hanging out with them. Some people will say, "Oh, I am strong enough to handle it". No, you are not! Jesus didn't hang out with everybody. He didn't hang out with the Pharisees and Sadducees.

As Christians, we are called to be kind to everybody. We should win every person that we can to Jesus Christ. Whoever you talk to or text, they are making impartations into your spirit. Be careful with who you allow to impart into your spirit. I believe many believers have limited their finances, their intellect, and their spiritual growth because they are unequally yoked with the wrong people.

I am going to give you three levels of relationships and then unpack them. First, you need someone who speaks into you. Secondly, you need someone that you speak to on your level. Thirdly, you need someone that you speak into. Let's unpack the first step you need someone who speaks into you. This is the mentor and mentee relationship; someone who mentors you. The Biblical word is discipleship, and the secular word is mentoring.

Elijah said to him, "Stay here Elisha; the Lord has sent me to Jericho." And he replied, "As surely as the Lord lives and as you live. I will not leave you." So they went to Jericho. The company of the prophets at Jericho went up to Elisha and asked him, "Do you know that the Lord is going to take your master from you today?" "Yes, I know," he replied, "so be quiet." Then Elijah said to him, "Stay here; the Lord has sent me to the Jordan." And he replied, "As surely as the Lord lives and as you live, I will not leave you." So, the two of them walked on.

2 Kings 2:4-6

I cannot presuppose that you know this story, but I would suggest that you read this whole story between Elijah and Elisha. I cannot unpack the whole story, but I will draw some Kingdom nuggets from it. This is the story of Elijah and Elisha. Don't get the "jah" and the "sha" mixed up. Elijah is the daddy (mentor), and Elisha is the son (mentee). Elijah is the one who did the discipling, and Elisha is the one being discipled or mentored. Elisha said to Elijah, "I'm not going to allow you to leave me because you are the one who speaks into my life, and wherever you go I am going because I have a divine connection with you."

Have you figured out yet that if this Kingdom element is not right, nothing else is right? As a pastor, I am that person to every single person in my congregation because I speak into their lives. When I speak of speaking into other's lives, I am talking about the things of God and not just limited to that but inclusive of that. My relationship with the members of the church is one of a mentor and mentee. I mentor and speak into them. Don't you minimize the church you go to. Don't minimize who your pastor and covering is because you are availing yourself to allow that man or woman of God to speak into you. I understand that each week the congregants of the church that I pastor give me two to three hours of their life every week by allowing me to pour the Word of God into them. I don't take that for granted, and that's why I come prepared, prayed up, anointed, and live right. I do not get back from them what I give, and I am not supposed to because that is not their role. They know that I speak into their lives and not the other way around.

The Spirit gives life; the flesh profits nothing. The words that I speak to you are spirit, and they are life.

John 6:63 (NKJV)

Right now, I am speaking life into you. Jesus said His Word is Spirit and life. People who are not getting God's Word are dying spiritually. If you're in a dead church where you are not being taught, you are dying with that church. The Word will impregnate you, challenge you, encourage you, and change your life. Most importantly, the Word will change you! Proverbs 18:21(a) says, *"Death and life are in the power of the tongue."* Words have power, and some people can kill you softly. They may ask, "Why are you still at that church?" or "Why are you there every time the doors open?" or "Why do you give your tithes over there?" They are killing you softly. It is impossible to hang with negative people and remain positive. They will contaminate you. Negativity and stress impact you. I am not telling you to go home and to cut everybody off, especially, if it's your spouse.

Let me give you a medical fact. Stress releases certain toxins that can age you and cause sickness. Even after the episode is over, the toxins remain in your body for at least 24 hours. So, the argument is over, but the toxins that got released are still impacting your body. So, we didn't know that the cause of death was that he was hanging out with the wrong friends? Maybe, this is too heavy for you. The death was caused by the crazy people that you keep letting into your life.

I call heaven and earth to witness against you today, that I have set before you life and death, the blessing and the curse. So choose life in order that you may live, you and your descendants.

Deuteronomy 30:19

God has placed certain people in your life, but you can choose to have people that speak life or death. Now, don't keep texting, emailing, or calling because of some loyalty from years ago or something that is irrelevant that's in your past. For instance, maybe you have someone that did something for you or they are a relative of yours. Remember in Matthew 12:46-50 (NKJV), when Jesus' mother and his brothers were outside, they said, *"Jesus, your Mom is outside."* Jesus said, *"Who is My mother and my brothers?"* No disrespect to Mary, but Jesus is saying, "Mary thinks that I'm her son, but it's now time for me to be her Savior." In perspective, Jesus is saying that the Kingdom is more important than any earthly relationship in the world. Don't let your relationships keep you away from God whether it's your dad, mom, sister, brother, or friend. You have to let God be true.

Paul discipled Timothy, Moses discipled Joshua, and Elijah discipled Elisha. It is my prayer that you grow spiritually. There is more in you than you are currently producing. When you conquer one thing, move to the next one. When you get over one issue, I want you to say, "Alright, I got that...let's get this together." Before you know it, you are going to be in shape, have a pocket full of money, your brain will be straight, have a good marriage, a nice house, and walk in the spirit. Why can't you have the full package? God says, "All things are possible if you only believe."

How do you grow? You grow in three ways. First, you grow through God's Word. Secondly, you grow through experience. Lastly, you grow through exposure. Second Peter 3:18 (NKJV) says, *"But grow in grace and truth and knowledge of our Lord and Savior Jesus Christ."* Grow in grace. Don't just have grace, but grow in grace. Grow in it!

Grow in God's Grace

Churches are a spiritual hospital; not a museum. I can assure you that the nurses and doctors who work at a hospital do not get upset and nervous because a patient has blood on them. That is the purpose that the hospital serves. Therefore, at a church, we cannot get nervous when people come in with issues. At the same time, if I have someone that has been with me a long time, by attending the church that I pastor, and they are not growing spiritually, if they can't get it straight with their spouse and if they are not tithing, then that becomes frustrating. If you attend a church on a regular basis, my question for you would be: "Why are you going if you're not growing in grace?" Let this Word do what it's intended to do in you. You may not be perfect, but go on and grow in God's grace.

Secondly, you grow through experience. There are some things that an institution cannot teach you. There are some things that life will teach you. Experience has taught you some things in life.

Thirdly, you grow by exposure. You cannot reach for what you have never seen. It is important to expose yourself to things. This book will stretch you beyond the same few people that you have been dealing with. Let me show you how to use your faith. Go to the car dealership and sit in the car that you want. Don't tell the car salesmen that you don't have any money. Just say, "Can I see the car please?" Another way to use your faith is by riding down the street you want to live on and say, "When we move here, I want this type of house with this type of furniture and this type of yard." Then, go and hangout with somebody that already has it [the car, the house, etc.]; so you can touch it, see it, and smell it.

Can I prophesy to you and tell you that God is expanding your vision. Your house is too small, your car doesn't cost enough, and your bank account doesn't have enough in it. You might not get rich, but you can have more than what you've got. God said, "I'm blessed." You can have money and be blessed because God's vision for your life is too big for you to be broke. If you're supposed to be broke then why did God give you such expensive taste? God put that inside of you because He's given you dominion. If you are a male, then you are a king. If you are a female, then you are a queen. You are a child of God. The Bible declares:

- Eyes have not seen... 2 Corinthians 2:9
- I pray that you may prosper and be in health even as your soul prospers 3 John 1:2
- The wealth of the wicked is laid up for the just... Proverbs 13:22
- God will make you the lender and not the borrower Proverbs 22:7
- But My God shall supply all of your needs! Philippians 4:19
- You are the head and not the tail! Deuteronomy 28:13
- I came that you might have life and have it more ... John 10:10

God wants to expose you not only financially, but He wants to expose you spiritually. An anonymous author said if you can read more than three pages in an hour then you are not really reading, because you should spend most of your time trying to figure out what the author is saying. Don't read those plastic romance novels that don't speak into your life. You are smarter than the way you are acting. A lot of what you don't have is because of you, leave the devil out of it. How many books do you read a year compared to how much TV do you watch? How much texting do you do? How much time do you spend on social media? Do you need someone to speak into you? You need to get exposed to something or someone that is greater than you.

Spiritual Guidance

First Samuel, Chapter 18 is the story of David and Jonathan. The Bible says that their souls were knit together. They were covenant brothers, and they had a friendship covenant. You need a person that speaks into you spiritually. In my life, that person is Bishop Dale C. Bronner. I am loyal to Bishop Dale C. Bronner because he speaks into my life. If I'm your pastor, then that would be me. If you attend another local church, then it would be your pastor or whoever else speaks into you and mentors you spiritually.

You need someone that speaks into you that is on the same level. There needs to be commonality. The first thing to have in common is Jesus Christ. Your best friend cannot be a sinner. I know he's your dog but tell Scooby Doo to get saved! How can a believer kick it with somebody who doesn't believe? Your best friend must be washed in the blood of the Lamb. Your best friend must have integrity or striving for it like you are. If you are married, then your best friend should be married. This relationship needs to symbiotic, I get something and you get something. In most relationships, somebody always gives more. It is never 50-50 giving. One of you gives more than the other, and the other one would like to get a little more. Symbiotic relationship means at least I get something as opposed to a relationship that is parasitic (parasite) and sucking the life out of you. This is the friend that you call and the entire conversation is about them. Don't hang with anybody that can't celebrate you. The Bible says, *"Can two walk together, except they be agreed?"* (Amos 3:3 KJV)

Now, you need someone that you can speak into. You have now moved to the place of mentoring. Who are you mentoring? This person is a positive person but they don't know enough for you to get anything out of the relationship. They are your assignment. They're a good person, but they don't know as much as you. They don't have what you've got. They are in your life for you to give, not for you to receive from.

Chapter Eight
Three Levels of Relationships

_____

_____

_____

_____

_____

_____

_____

_____

_____

_____

_____

_____

_____

_____

Chapter Nine

I Won't Run Out!

A certain woman of the wives of the sons of the prophets cried out to Elisha, saying, "Your servant my husband is dead, and you know that your servant feared the Lord. And the creditor is coming to take my two sons to be his slaves." So Elisha said to her, "What shall I do for you? Tell me, what do you have in the house?" And she said, "Your maidservant has nothing in the house but a jar of oil."

2 Kings 4:1-2 (NKJV)

No matter how difficult this year has been financially for America, we as believers have to remain confident as sons and daughters of God that we won't run out! God has a plan for His people. The passage in 2 Kings 4:1-2 indicates that a widow faced a severe and urgent crisis. The widow's husband who was a prophet had died and left her with a lot of debt. She didn't have the money to pay her creditors. Apparently, her husband was not an ascetic prophet, which means no sex, no money, no wife, just Jesus. If her husband were an ascetic prophet, he would have been into Monasticism, a monastery, or would have been a monk. Apparently, this was no ascetic, monasticism school of prophets where all they did was pray all day. These prophets had wives.

The prophet had a wife, and even though he is in ministry, he did not prepare for the future. The prophet was preaching and died with no insurance, as a result, the creditors were threatening to enslave his two sons. In America, no matter how many people you owe, there is no one threatening to come and take your children to make them slaves. However, in Jewish custom, whoever you owed had the right to come get you and your children so that all of you could become workers for them; not slaves. You would become a worker or a servant until either the debt was paid or until Jubilee. The widow uses the word "slave" because people have a tendency of taking advantage of the marginalized.

I believe that God blesses you to bless someone else. If you study Christology, you will notice that whenever you see Jesus, He is hanging with poor people trying to help them get themselves together. God didn't educate you and bless you with a nice house in the suburbs just for you to say, "I made it." God wants every one of us to make it, but shame on you if you don't go back to help the marginalized and the poor. The text says that the widow doesn't have anything, but she cried out! She could have sat back and not done anything, but she said, "It's not my time to die." Maybe you're saying, "I know I'm going to die, but I'm not dying today." You have decided that you're not going to let the stuff from your past stop what God is getting ready to do in your life right now.

What's in Your Possession?

The text says, "She cried out." The widow's husband was a godly man, but now, she is situated in extreme poverty. She is utterly destitute with no food and no supplies but the Bible says,

"She cried out!" The Bible doesn't give the widow's name, but we do know that her husband is gone and they are about to take both of her sons, but she says, "No, I am going to cry out!" To cry out really means to make a faith move. The widow lost her husband and she's broke, but she refuses to adapt to the poverty mindset that leads to mediocrity. The woman cried out! She cried out as if it were to mean, "I've got to try something!" That's what her actions reflected. So, the widow cried out to the prophet Elisha. According to the scriptures, the widow tells Elisha that they are coming to get her babies. She tells him that she doesn't have any money and that his prophet (her husband) loved him. In 2 Kings 4:2, Elisha said to her, *"What shall I do for you? Tell me, what do you have in the house?"* The widow replied, *"Your maidservant has nothing in the house but a jar of oil."*

So, let me make my point. Don't just tell me what you have lost, but tell me what you still have! Don't' just talk about what the devil has done, but talk about what God is doing in your life right now. It's important that you deal with your losses, at some point. No matter how tragic the loss, you have to get up! I lost both of my parents 14 months apart, but once you deal with the loss, get up! You cannot stay down the rest of your life no matter who left you, who divorced you, who molested you, or who fired you. You have to decide that the devil is a liar, and you better get yourself together because you are too blessed to be stressed.

Elisha's job description said: I help people to get up! He helped people get up from abandonment, abuse, ignorance, dumb relationships, lack of love, no joy, and no peace. I don't care how low a man is, if somebody preaches the Kingdom of God into him, he'll get up. No matter how dark it gets, Christ will get you up! As much as I love you in Christ, I cannot stay down with you. You may say, "Bishop, my spouse let me down." or "The person I thought I was going to marry walked away." My response is, "I'm sorry. Go ahead and cry, then, get up!"

Elisha said (verse 2, paraphrased), *"Girl, what's in this house? Show me what you're working with."* What gifts and talents do you possess? What do you do for a living? Have you perfected that? Are you the best in your department? What's in the house? Don't tell me what you have lost, instead, tell me what you have left. Don't tell me where you've been, but tell me where you want to go. Don't even tell me about your horrific past, but let's discuss your fantastic future. What do you have in the house? Elisha says (verse 1-2, paraphrased), *"Lady, you stopped me. I was just walking by, and I heard you say something about losing your husband. What do you want to do? What do you have in the house?"* The widow responds, *"I don't have anything in the house but..."* Either you have something or you don't. The widow minimized what she had.

Most believers minimize what they have. They don't realize that God doesn't need much because He divides and then He multiplies. Elisha is asking, "What do you have? What are you willing to release to God to let Him work with?" In 2 Kings 4:3 (NKJV) Elisha says, *"Go, borrow vessels from everywhere, from all your neighbors-empty vessels; do not gather just a few."* In other words, your little is about to become much! Say, "I'm shouting for what I have, and I am shouting for what I am about to get." Elisha tells her to tell both of her sons to go around the hood and gather every empty vessel they can. In verse 4, Elisha says (paraphrased), *"And shut the door behind you."* Why does she have to shut the door? Shutting the door represents that everyone cannot handle what God is about to do in your life. People don't need to see you while you are in process because they will hate on your process. They don't have to see the process, but they will see the results. When God gets through with you all they will have to say is, "There is a God!"

Your Get Up Season

In verse 5 (paraphrased) the widow says, *"I don't know what God is doing, but I'm going to trust Him."* Some scholars think that the oil was cooking oil, but another scholar says that it's the same oil that the woman with the alabaster box had. The purpose of the alabaster oil was to preserve the body after it died. The alabaster oil served as a burial ointment, which suggests that the widow was saying, "All I have is enough to die with." This means that she was stuck in a posture of poverty.

The first thing I have to do is to get you to think differently. As you're reading this book, I want you to change your thinking because if you believe that you can get up, your body and your money will soon follow.

After Elisha tells the widow to get the vessels, he tells her to take all the oil that she has and to start pouring. The text says that the widow took the oil and began to pour and oil turned into oil. The widow started pouring oil into one vessel but the oil would not stop running. Oil was coming out of the oil. God is just making a way! In verse 6 (paraphrased), the widow tells her son, *"Bring me those empty vessels!"* If you are not careful, sometimes your family will miss the move of God. It is your responsibility to speak into their life and tell them to bring you the vessels. Then, one of the boys says (verse 6 paraphrased), *"Mom, we don't have anymore vessels."* The Bible says that the oil stopped.

You Won't Run Out!

When God is pouring out, all you have to do is keep giving God something to work with. "Bishop, how do I become a millionaire?" You must start with a millionaire vision. Money doesn't come; money waits. When the widow's son told her that they had no more vessels, the oil stopped. It was though she was saying, "Since you don't have anything for me to pour into, I won't waste the oil." Oil is a type of spirit. When you tithe, you are not going to run out. I know some good Christians who ran out. Sometimes your money may get low, and that's life, but God will step in just when you need Him the most.

Let me give you four things that you won't run out of if you are sold out to Him.

1. Your peace will not run out, because God will keep you in perfect peace whose mind is stayed on Him (Isaiah 26:3). He is the Prince of Peace.
2. You won't run out of His presence. If your mother, spouse, or friend leaves you, there's a reason. God has got you all by yourself so he could talk to you by yourself.
3. You won't run out of joy.

4. You won't run out of reasons to praise Him.

If you can't praise Him for what He's doing right now, I dare you to praise Him on credit! If He brought you out of anything, don't sit there like a frog on a log. Let everything that has breath praise the Lord! I won't run out of praise. If you tithe, you will live right. If you fast for Him, then you won't run out of money. He will make a way out of no way. Don't say I've run out. You didn't run out; you just didn't trust God. You may have spent your money on the wrong things but through all of that He's still keeping you.

The prophet asked the woman to do something, and I'm asking you to do something; keep moving. The time you spend texting, you could be writing your book. The time you spend watching TV, you could be finishing your bachelor's degree or your business degree.

Chapter Nine
I Won't Run Out!

So Goes the Woman
Reflections by Pastor Anita F. Jackson

So Goes the Woman   **Chapter Seven**

The Fever is Broken

Bishop stated that no matter what things look like in your life, you have to learn to trust God. Trust Him even with the tithe. Bishop said that even with your unemployment check, if all you have is $20 … tithe. We have heard it said that little becomes much when you place it in the Master's hand. Bishop and I know this to be true. We have been in that place where all we could do was trust God. Yet, we kept on tithing. When you keep on tithing, what seems impossible, God will make possible! We can truly stand on Psalm 23 and Galatians 6:9.

So Goes the Woman   **Chapter Eight**

Three Levels of Relationships

Bishop talked about the relationship between Elijah and Elisha, the mentor and the mentee. The mentor is the one who speaks into your life. Bishop speaks into my life and into the life of our children. I watch him study the Word of God for hours at a time as he prepares to deliver the Word on Sunday mornings and Wednesday nights. I have learned that time alone with God should be top priority in my life. We were created to have fellowship with God. We learn that time alone with God will give us the words to say to others. The relationship that you have with God will help you in your relationship with people. Grow in God's grace. We have learned that the church is a spiritual hospital and that people are really (spiritually) sick in so many different ways.

We should be able to speak life, provide spiritual guidance to people. John 6:63 (NKJV) says *"The Spirit gives life; the flesh profits nothing. The words that I speak to you are spirit and they are life."* Speak life into someone.

So Goes the Woman   # Chapter Nine

I Won't Run Out!

This chapter blessed me! The widow cried out. I have cried out. The widow was going through a hard time. She had lost her husband, but she had a jar and some oil. With this, she made a "faith move". The widow did not give up so that means that we can't give up. God's providential hand is always at work in our life. God sent a prophet, Elisha. This tells me that I am never alone, forgotten, or abandoned. Jesus is beside me and Bishop. David wrote in Psalm 23:4, *"Even though I walk through the valley of the shadow of death, I fear no evil, for You are with me."* I can struggle or do like the widow and turn it over to the Lord. God will take care of our needs. The widow made a faith move; she took the oil and began to pour. The oil turned into oil; the oil would not stop running. I can hear Bishop say, "Go on and praise God like you already have it!"

Part IV

A New Creation in Christ

Chapter Ten

Raise Your Level of Expectation

I try to spend a lot of my time in life with this "Kaleo" on my life focusing on men. I know if you catch the man, you have to catch a fish before you can clean it, if you catch the man he will go back and catch his family and get his whole family cleaned up with Jesus. That's how it works. If we as men would take on this spiritual responsibility, 1 Corinthians 2:14 (NKJV) tells us, *"But the natural man does not receive the things of the Spirit of God, for they are foolishness to him; nor can he know them, because they are spiritually discerned."*

The world has a lot of men punked out, I don't know any better way to put it, thinking that to be a Christian man is sissified. That is a lie straight from the pits of Hell. A real man is a godly man, he is a Kingdom man, and he walks in Kingdom authority. One of the worst things we did back in the day was to be with a bunch of girls. That is one of the worst things a man can do. Paul called that the most destructive sin. Most men wait in life until it's too late. You need to grab this now.

Let this mind be in you which was also in Christ Jesus.

Philippians 2:5

When you have the mind of Christ, you realize that Christ has your situation under His control. Say, "Christ has my situation under control." When you gave your life to Christ, He didn't add

His mind on top of your old thinking. 2 Corinthians 5:17 (NKJV) says, *"Therefore if anyone is in Christ, he is a new creation; old things are passed away; behold all things have become new."* You are not who you use to be. So Goes the Man, So Goes the Family.

Most Christian men, we do not have clarity of our assignment of who we are in Christ, and here is why, it is the Father's responsibility to speak into the life of the son to tell him who he really is in life. That is the primary role of a father. The primary role of a father is to speak into the life of his son and sons and tell them who they are in Christ Jesus. So Goes the Man, So Goes the Family.

This is why a bunch of men sleep around. The reason a bunch of them sleep around is because they don't know who they are. Many of them did not have their relationship in tact early on in life with their mom so they are still looking for momma. Thank God for momma. I would not be preaching the gospel if it were not for my mom and my grandmother. I know that. I realize that. They snatched me. You do not wait until a child gets in middle school or high school to try to get them on track in life. Christ needs to be every man's platform. If Christ is not your platform, you are going to get into this relationship, go from this career, you will be doing this, and you will be unstable for the rest of your days. By the way, you do not have to work on Sundays now. If you're volunteering to work on Sundays, that is out of order. Don't send your family to church; you come with your family.

My grandson, Edward will be two and a half in the month of August. Already, I am speaking things into his life just as I did with my son, Getties Jr. early on. I am speaking it into Edward's life. I am telling him who he is in Christ. Edward loves to get my iPhone and listen to his grandpa preach. When I pull my phone, he's clapping. He wants it. You have to start early. This is not a game. We have to know what the will of Christ is for us. Declare this over your situation:

Christ has the situation under His control. Because I am submitted to Christ, He controls my life. Christ controls my marriage, my family, my healing, and my mind. I have the mind of Christ!

Celebrate on that. You don't have a nasty mind; you have the very mind of Christ.

Jesus came to give you abundance in your home, body, workplace, family, and finances. So Goes the Man, So Goes the Family. Recently, I had a pastors and first ladies' roundtable. One of the things that I brought out in the meeting is that it is not the woman that is the problem, it's the man. The man does not know who he is yet. Because if he knows who he is, he can go back and get her straighten out in Jesus' name. If she's godly, she does not want to be the man. A real woman does not want to be the head. It's too much!

Jesus says in John 10:10, *"The thief comes to steal, kill, and destroy. I have come that you may have life and have it more abundantly."* For men, we are the priest, prophet, and king over our homes. If you are not born again, you cannot be the priest, prophet, and king. I've never met a nasty priest. I've never met a nasty prophet. I've never met a filthy, nasty king. Say, "Priest, prophet, and king of my home." It is important for us to renew our mind everyday, throughout the day. Say this, "It's time for me to renew my mind with the Word of God." The reason I want you to say these things because if you start saying them then automatically in your cognitive domain, you are going to raise your level of thinking. Haven't you figured this thing out that this sleeping around is empty? Haven't your figured out that this nasty stuff going with this one or that one is empty? Haven't you figured out yet that "thing" whatever it is can't fulfill you? Haven't you figured out that can't nobody do you like Jesus? No one can do you like Jesus. Absolutely, no one!

We should hear the conclusion of the whole matter rather than limit God to what He wants to do in our lives. Most men have not heard the whole conclusion of the matter because we think it's about looking at sexy women and sports. No, it is not about that. You missed it. You missed it big. Most of you are probably old enough to realize, "That's stuff empty, Bishop." That's what I am trying to tell you. God has given you the ability to be in control of every circumstance and situation that occurs in your life. Learn to speak to your social, financial, physical, spiritual, and emotional situation. Take those bills as silly as it may look in the natural, spread them on the table at home, and speak to them. Tell those bills, "According to the Word of God, Philippians 4:19 (NKJV) teach us, *'And my God shall supply all your needs according to His riches in glory by Christ Jesus.'*" Speak to the bills. Say, "I call you, debt, paid in full. There won't be any bankruptcy in this bloodline. Debt, I call you paid in full. Thank you, Lord Jesus right now that I've got more than enough. Hallelujah. I've got plenty more to put in store." Are we faith people? Who are we then? Faith people should speak faith. Not all this other stuff, "I don't know how I'm going to do it." I do. Shout, "The devil is a liar, and Jesus Christ is supplying all of my needs according to His riches in glory by Christ."

How can you do this? You can achieve this through the Word of God and by faith. Look man, that's how you speak to it. A real man is a Kingdom man. A real man is filled with the Holy Ghost. A real man does not cheat on his wife. A real godly man is not a player. No, the devil is a liar. Hallelujah. There's stuff in the bloodline, and God raised you up to pull that stuff up by the roots that you will not be a player, your sons will not be a player, and your grandsons will not be a player. You have got to speak to this thing in the name of Jesus. If you do not stop it, then it might not be stopped.

Stop being passive to your wife. Stop saying things like, "Yes, ma'am. Ok." No, you're the man! Stop saying things like, "What do you want me to do now? Do you want me to jump? How high do you want me to jump? These britches aren't ok? I"ll just get some more. Are these ok?" No, you're the man! You have to know who you are. You've got to figure out who you are. Ok, just keep living how you're living, and you are going to get into a train wreck - a plane will crash in your life. You may walk away. You may lose it all. You better thank God that we serve a God of another chance.

I am coming across hard because you cannot play with a man. A man has to be told who he is in Christ. Most of us were told to spread all of our wild oats when we were young. That's the worst thing that you can tell a man or a young boy. Don't you know that there is a consequence for every action? Don't you know when you have these wrong choices how embarrassing it is? When you are married and your child says, "Oh, Daddy, I have another brother?" Your response may be, "Yes, he's in Florida.", "Yes, he's in California.", "Yes, he's up in Ohio.", or "Yes, he's up in Jersey." Do you see how painful that is? Now, take care of baby but don't do it again. Don't do it again. It's [sex] not free. In the state of South Carolina, they will lock you up if you don't' pay. They will lock you up quicker for that than for killing people. Oh, you're going to jail. I'll come see you when I can, but you wouldn't listen. You wouldn't listen. Your head's hard, can't tell you anything. I am trying to tell you, "When are you going to marry her?" I love you but you cannot date her forever. Ya'll been dating for 10 years. Ten years!!

I knew back in 9th or 10th grade, in high school, that I would have daughters one day. I knew then. I wasn't getting this teaching, but I was raised right. There were girls back then that I told, "I can't do that to you." I wasn't even a Christian then. I knew it was wrong. I knew my heart was not in that. I knew that all I would be doing would be using them. So, I knew what goes around, comes back around. What goes up comes back down. It is called the Law of Reciprocity. *"God is not mocked; for whatever a man sows, that he shall also reap"* Galatians 6:7 (NKJV). Sin will take you further than you want to go, keep you longer than you want to stay, and will cost you, more than you want to pay. Sin will. See, you think it is cute. You say, "What's up girl? Come here, we need to get together." Remember, sin will take you further than you want to go, keep you longer than you want to stay. You want to come out it, and you can't get out of it. "What does this mean, Bishop?" I'll tell you what it means. The devil has his claws in you, and he cannot let you go until God says, "Enough is enough!" You may be saying, "Bishop, I've got this thorn." Paul did also. What's your problem? Paul went on to write two-thirds of the New Testament. Every man has a thorn. I've got a thorn. Everybody's got a thorn. It's the thorn that is going to keep you praying. It's that thorn that going to make you walk by faith.

In Romans 8:37, Paul calls us, *"More than conquerors."* Say, "I'm more than a conqueror." That means there is nothing in your bloodline that when the blood of Jesus is on you that can hold you back, that can stop you. Are you getting this? It cannot stop you. Not even a generational curse. Say, "I am more than a conqueror." Here's the picture. That thing that had you pinned down, you are now looking at it in the face, and you are now conquering it. Generational curses, conqueror that! Lying, conqueror that! Broke all the time, conqueror that! Poverty mind set, conqueror that! Are you getting this? You and I are heirs to the Lord's promises. Romans 8:17(a) says, *"And if children, then heirs; heirs of God, and joint-heirs with Christ."* Speak to your situation by faith and say, "I am living the abundant life!" Put poverty, sickness, addictions, marital problems, rebellious children, and unemployment on notice. How? By speaking to it. Declare this right now in Jesus' name:

I have an anointing on my life that knows everything about me. I have to succeed in life! Jesus is the vine, and I am one of the branches. I have to stay connected to God because He is my source!

Control Your Tongue

You have received a fresh revelation from God. His Word is a lamp unto your feet and a light unto your path (Psalm 119:105). Our words are vital to bringing our dreams to pass. It's not enough to see it by faith or in your imagination. You have to begin speaking words of faith over your life and know that Jesus came to give you the abundant life. The moment you speak something you give birth to it because words are spiritual. The spiritual principle works whether what you're saying is good, bad, positive, or negative. Your problem is you have been going around blaming everybody else, but the truth is that you are your own worst enemy. You may say, "See, my daddy wasn't in my life. My momma didn't treat me right." You are a grown man. It's time to man up. It's time to be the man that God has called you to be. The scripture says, *"We are snared by the word of our mouth"* (Proverbs 6:2). You are taken by the words you speak. For example, you may say things like, "I can't do anything right", or "I knew I wouldn't get the promotion." Your tongue keeps tripping you up and preventing you from moving ahead in life. You have a tongue problem. This is why you must learn to guard your tongue and speak faith-filled words over your life. Your words will make you or break you. God told me to tell you to stop talking about your pain and suffering! Instead, speak constantly of His goodness. Learn to speak His promises at the breakfast table, at lunch, and at dinner. Stop talking about the negative things, and begin to talk about God's Word. Stop talking about the problem, and start talking about the solution.

If you are married, the reason your wife is acting crazy is because you are crazy. Get in your place, and don't focus on her even if she is not involved in your life. My wife is major in my life and I am talking major, major, major. It makes me feel like I can conqueror anything. If you look at your wife as just a woman, you are missing it. If you look at your wife as if you can't tell her anything, I love you but that is stupid. I didn't call you stupid but I said that is stupid. If you don't include her, you are missing what God has for you in the Word of God. That's why the Word of God says when a man finds a wife, he finds a good thing and he obtains favor (Refer to Proverbs 18:22). My wife is my favor.

Every major thing that I've done in life, after God has showed it to me, after I have prayed about it, I bring it to my wife because godly women have a way of birthing things. You are sharing it with all of your buddies, and you should be sharing it with your favor. There is nothing in my life even when my mother was alive that I put before my wife. I was a momma's boy. There is no man alive who has been closer to his mother than me. We might be neck and neck but I'm a momma's boy. I never put my mom before my wife because I knew what the Word of God said. My daughters could tell you. The most important person on planet earth is not the church, not my children, not my mother-in law and my father-in law, but my wife. You keep stuff quiet from your wife. You include everybody else but her. Have you lost your everlasting mind? That's your favor! Your wife will be there for you when your momma's not speaking to you. She'll be there for you when your mother doesn't feel you. That's bone of your bone, that's flesh of your flesh. That's your favor. She's not just your woman. That's your wife. She is to be honored.

You've been dating her for 10 years. You don't even know her yet, and she doesn't know you. You may say, "I don't know about that, Bishop." I do. The day you get married, you'll think that she flipped on you. She didn't flip. She's just letting the truth come out now. She'll say, "I never did like bowling." You will be like, "You don't like bowling. You went with me every week." Let her turn her head on her shoulders seven times. You're anointed to handle that. She's going to flip on you.

Do not use words to describe your situation; instead, use words to change your situation. You have the Word of God in your mouth, and if you speak to your situation; God will change your situation. He will change every circumstance, situation, problem, and trial that you will ever face. He wants to supply you with the finances to pay every bill. He wants you to have wisdom, knowledge, patience, joy, faith, humility, and longsuffering to handle anything that might come your way. When evil thoughts try to attack your mind, God has given you His Word to renew your mind. When sickness and disease try to attack your body, His Word is a medicine chest to raise your body up again. *"[God's Word] will be healing to your body and refreshment to your bones"* (Refer to Proverbs 3:8). When the enemy comes into your life and tries to cause separation and divorce, God has given you His

Word to speak to your marriage, and God will change it! I do not care if your marriage turns into a rock. If you will speak to it, that rock will transform. Your marriage will transform. Not everything you went through in your marriage was for you, it was for another couple, and in fact, it was for a whole lot of couples that is why God allowed you and your wife to go through it. You don't have anything to be ashamed of. Thank God that He gave you another chance. You don't look like what you been through. You can tell others, "All you see is my glory, but you don't know my real story."

You are the standard. God raised you up to make a difference in your bloodline. While you are looking at your Uncle, Dad or others, God raised you up to be the real deal. You are a Kingdom man, you are anointed and you are more than enough. As a matter of fact, El Shaddai abides on the inside of you, and the devil knows, "I just can't let him figure out why he is going through all the stuff that he's ever been through in life." Look, you're going to make an impact. Shout, "Hallelujah." Shout, "Now is the time for the saints of the Most High to rise up and possess the Kingdom."

If your husband or future husband is not much, I'm going to tell you why he's not much, it's because you do not put a demand on him. You have to put a demand on him. My wife puts pressure on me. She makes me perform. She puts a demand on me. As his wife, you have to say things like, "No, not on my watch, baby. You are more than that. You can do all things through Christ. I am so proud of you, and I thank God for you. I know that the Word of God says according to Jeremiah 29:11 (KJV), *'For I know the thoughts that I think toward you, saith the Lord, thoughts of peace, and not of evil, to give you an expected end.'* Oh, we're going to be out of debt. No, there's not going to be any bankruptcy. We're going to be out of debt. No, we are not going to be in debt up to here. In the near future, we are going to live like we've never lived. We're going to drive like we've never driven. We've going to love like we've never loved." You may ask, "Bishop, how does a man of God do that?" Go back and start doing those things that won her. You have to know how to make her blush; make her smile. Tell her how much you love her. Tell her how much you believe in her, and watch how God starts elevating your life. Meditate on the verse that says, *"What God has joined together, let no man put asunder"* (Matthew 19:6). If you learn to speak that you're living the abundant life, you are telling your situation what to do instead of your situation telling you.

The Spirit of the Lord is upon Me because He has anointed Me to heal the broken hearted. To preach deliverance to the captives and recovering of sight to the blind, to set at liberty to them that are bruised, to preach the acceptable year of the Lord.

Isaiah 61:1

Change Your Thinking

There's an anointing on you that brokenness can't stay on you. God's placed an anointing on you that sickness cannot stay in you or in your household. Once you get the house right, then you can go tell others, in the bloodline, and at church, "Don't bash prosperity." You can tell them that. It is not the will of God for you to be broke. What can two broke people do together but pray? Doesn't it feel better when you have some money in your pocket? You have to know what's at stake.

Everybody comes from something. As a wife, you have to push your husband like my wife pushes me. Here is the thing about a man. If he is not working, there is a strong possibility that he is that close to going back to doing the stuff he knows is not right. He is that close to going back to hanging with those wrong friends.

Men, there's an anointing on your life. Tomorrow morning, like in baseball or in softball, I want you to aim for the fence. Say, "Ya'll can come if you want to, but I'm aiming for the fence." That's the way it should be in your life as a man of God. You may say, "Bishop, my wife is fussing too much." You know why she's fussing so much, let's go back to Genesis, Adam after he started compromising he forgot the clarity of his assignment, he forgot who he was. His wife [Eve] went and handed him a snake. When your wife is frustrated, no telling what she'll bring you. It is your responsibility to say, "Nothing ungodly will be in this house." Are you getting this?

Jesus walks on the pages in the fourth chapter of Luke and says, "I'm anointed to preach the gospel to the poor." He said, "I've got the anointing for the broken so that he doesn't have to have the broken-hearted any longer." Jesus also says, "I've got the anointing to preach deliverance to the captives." Learn to think on your level of anointing. Don't let your mind talk you out of your destiny. We need prosperity because some people are broke. We need salvation because some people are lost. We need healing because some people are sick. We need deliverance because some people are in bondage.

Reject the enemy's thoughts. God's dream for your life is much bigger than you can imagine. If God showed you everything He has in store for you, it would blow your mind. There is no such thing in the Kingdom of God as low class or fixed income. Are you limiting God? When God puts a dream in your heart, do you step boldly in faith or do you step back in fear and say, "That's too big for me.", "I'm not qualified.", "I'm not able.", or "I could never do that." God wants to do a new thing in your life, but you have to do your part and get outside of that little box. Stop settling for little. Stop saying, "I don't have enough education." Stop saying, "I'll never make much more than I am now." Listen to me, your job is not your source, God is! I have come to a place in my life to expect God's supernatural increase and promotion. We often get comfortable with where we are, and we use that as an excuse to remain in the place of lack. We say things like, "No one in my blood line ever amounted to much so I guess I won't either." Don't believe that lie. God is a promotional God, and He wants you to break that "Spirit of poverty mold".

Learn to raise your level of expectation. You have to change your thinking before you can change your living. Program your mind for success. Everyday, you should choose to live with an attitude that expects good things to happen to you. The Bible says, *"Set your mind and keep it set on higher things"* (Colossians 3:2). When you get up in the morning, you should set your mind in the right direction. Say something like, "This is going to be a great day because the Lord is guiding my steps! His favor is

Bishop Getties L. Jackson, Sr. *So Goes The Man, So Goes The Family*

surrounding me. Goodness and mercy are following me. I am excited about today!"

Chapter Ten
Raise Your Level of Expectation

_____

_____

_____

_____

_____

_____

_____

_____

_____

_____

_____

_____

_____

_____

_____

Chapter Eleven

You Can't Die, You Must Survive This!

Everyone knows about the great actor Robin Williams who recently passed. Always remember than when someone like him dies in the way that he did, suffering from manic depression, it affects everyone. I would like to share with you the news report concerning this.

San Rafael, Calif. (AP) — Robin Williams' personal assistant found the actor who was struggling with depression dead in a bedroom of his San Francisco Bay Area home, officials said Tuesday. Williams was last seen alive by his wife Sunday night when she went to bed, according to Lt. Keith Boyd, chief deputy coroner for the Marin County Sheriff's office. She woke up the next morning and left, thinking he was still asleep elsewhere in the house. Shortly after, Williams' personal assistant came to the home and became concerned when Williams failed to respond to knocks at a door. The assistant found the 63-year-old actor clothed and dead in a bedroom. Boyd said all evidence indicates Williams, star of "Good Will Hunting," "Mrs. Doubtfire," "Good Morning, Vietnam," and dozens of other films, committed suicide by hanging himself with a belt. But Boyd said a final ruling will be made once toxicology reports and interviews with witnesses are complete.

The condition of the body indicated Williams had been dead for at least a few hours, Boyd said. Williams also had superficial cuts on his wrist, and a pocketknife was found nearby. Williams had been seeking treatment for depression, Boyd said. Boyd would not say whether the actor left a suicide note. The Oscar-winning actor for years dealt with bouts of substance abuse and depression and referenced his struggles in his comedy routines. Just last month, Williams announced he was returning to a 12-step treatment program. Experts stressed that suicide is rarely triggered by a single factor such as depression or substance abuse. Typically, there are at least two such influences, often compounded by acute stress, such as financial hardship or troubled personal relationships.

"Yesterday, I lost my father and a best friend and the world got a little grayer," Williams' son Zak said in a statement. "I will carry his heart with me every day. I would ask those that loved [my dad] to remember him by being as gentle, kind, and generous as he would be. Seek to bring joy to the world as [my dad] sought."

Makeshift memorials of flowers and notes popped up around the country including on Williams' star on the Hollywood Walk of Fame, at his home, and outside the house where the '80s sitcom "Mork & Mindy" was set in Boulder, Colorado. People also gathered to remember Williams at a bench in Boston's Public Garden where he filmed a scene for "Good Will Hunting." Ben Affleck, a co-star and co-writer on that movie, was among the legions of friends and fans who shared tributes online. "Robin had a ton of love & did so much for so many," Affleck tweeted. "He made Matt & my dreams come true. What do you owe a guy who does that? Everything."

Robin Williams was loved by millions. If you are depressed, please get help. It's believed that 19 million Americans are depressed. We all have problems, but we all have this one area or issue that we need God to help us with now. Taking your life is not the solution to your problems.

In this chapter, I will focus on helping you deal with your problems and issues, but from the standpoint that it is already done. That is what faith is. Romans 4:17(b) (NKJV) says, *"[faith] calls those things which do not exist as though they did."* Hebrews 11:1 (NKJV) says, *"Now faith is the substance of things hoped for, the evidence of things not seen."* You cannot just say it, there has to be some effort and discipline behind it.

The Storm

When considerable time had passed and the voyage was now dangerous, since even the fast was already over, Paul began to admonish them, and said to them, "Men, I perceive that the voyage will certainly be with damage and great loss, not only of the cargo and the ship, but also of our lives." But the centurion was more persuaded by the pilot and the captain of the ship than by what was being said by Paul. Because the harbor was not suitable for wintering, the majority reached a decision to put out to sea from there, if somehow they could reach Phoenix, a harbor of

Crete, facing southwest and northwest, and spend the winter there.

Acts 27:9-12

When you make a decision to walk with God and to stick with God, the enemy comes at you with everything that he has. Don't you agree? There are areas in our life that before we came to Christ, the enemy didn't bother us. Part of that is because he had us mastered in those areas. But when we came to Christ, all of a sudden the enemy started bringing stuff up against us. The enemy will bring storms into your life to distract you and to try to keep you from getting to the next level, the next dimension, the next season in your life. The devil likes you when you are struggling, tripping, or upset.

In Acts Chapter 27, Paul is a prisoner. He is always being locked up for doing what is right. Whenever we see Paul, he is chained to somebody or in prison for the sake of the Gospel. Paul is on assignment to stand before Caesar and to give a testimony, but the devil does not want Paul to make it there because the devil does not want the Gospel spread.

Acts 27:9 says, *"When considerable time had passed and the voyage was now dangerous, since even the fast was already over, Paul began to admonish them."* The fast was probably the Day of Atonement which occurred in early September to late October. After a certain time of the year, sailing was hazardous, and sea traffic in or around the month of November would cease. It wasn't the season to move yet. God can promote you in your life even if it's not your season. God can promote you without anyone

- 154 -

knowing about it or without you announcing that it is your season. God is sovereign. He has all the power.

It is not even the season for sailing, yet the ship sails anyway. Now, they are in some crazy weather. Remember, Paul is not on the ship as a passenger. He is there as a prisoner but he's on the ship.

But not long after, a tempestuous head wind arose, called Euroclydon. So when the ship was caught, and could not head into the wind, we let her drive. And running under the shelter of an island called Clauda, we secured the skiff with difficulty. When they had taken it on board, they used cables to undergird the ship; and fearing lest they should run aground on the Syrtis Sands, they struck sail and so were driven. And because we were exceedingly tempest-tossed, the next day they lightened the ship. On the third day we threw the ship's tackle overboard with our own hands. Now when neither sun nor stars appeared for many days, and no small tempest beat on us, all hope that we would be saved was finally given up.

Acts 27:14-20 (NKJV)

According to the scripture, the storm was so violent that they gave up hope that they could survive it. Have you ever noticed that the closer you get to your destiny, the darker and cloudier it gets? The goal of the enemy is to send such a storm in your life that will cause you to forget where you are headed.

There are two types of storms. There are sinful storms and then there are sovereign storms. A sinful storm is when I'm doing something that I shouldn't be doing and the Lord disciplines me for it. A sovereign storm is when I'm living better than I've ever lived but I'm catching more hell than I've ever caught. A sovereign storm is also when God allows something to come into my life not because I have been disobedient but because I have been obedient. God will use that storm to get me closer to Him and to get me to the next level. When storms come into our life, some of us want to quit and abandon what has gotten us this far. You have come too far to turn around now.

The scripture says that the storm was so violent that the passengers had gone without food for a number of days. They had destroyed most of their supplies, and Paul, who is a prisoner on the ship, has to preach to the captain and the crew. Sometimes, you don't have a clue why God has you where He has you, but sometimes you've got to be the light in a dark place. Paul stands up and says, "Do not abandon the ship, because I had a vision." Paul says, "God spoke to me and said the reason I'm on the ship is because I have to get to Rome so that I can stand before Caesar. Therefore, the ship cannot go down while I'm on it. Because I'm on the ship and I can't die, you are about to get blessed too" (Refer to Acts 27:21-25). You are blessed. God told me to tell you that you cannot be broke anymore. God told me to tell you that your marriage is going to get better. Whatever your storm may be, you are not going to die in this storm!

Paul had two visions: Acts 18:9-10 (KJV) says, *"One night the Lord spoke to Paul in a vision: 'Do not be afraid; keep on speaking, do not be silent. For I am with you, and no one is going to attack and harm you, because I have many people in this city.'"*

Acts 23:11 (KJV) says, *"And the night following the Lord stood by him, and said, 'Be of good cheer, Paul: for as thou hast testified of me in Jerusalem, so must thou bear witness also at Rome.'"*

We also know that this is not the first time that Paul has been on a ship. The experiences that you have survived will give you your greatest testimonies. One of the reasons that God allowed you to survive was not so that you could become arrogant, but so that you could become a blessing to somebody else who is in the eye of the storm. This is why your test becomes a testimony. Since you have been through some stuff and have survived some stuff, you can tell somebody, "If I made it, and I did, then you can make it too."

Paul had two visions prior to this and those visions encouraged him. In Paul's Jerusalem vision, God promised Paul a safe journey to Rome. Acts 27:22 says, *"Yet now I urge you to keep up your courage, for there will be no loss of life among you, but only of the ship."* This means you will not die! You will not lose your mind, because I've got a Word from God and the Word is this - you are going to survive this storm.

In the midst of tough times, keep a good spirit. The devil is after your disposition. Never allow your disposition to be a reflection of what you're going through. Life is a trip! Just because things look bad, it doesn't mean I'm not going to look bad because this joy that I have, the world didn't give it to me and the world can't take it away!

Stay on the Ship!

The storm was so bad that they wanted to jump off the ship, and they started letting down the little boats. Have you ever been on a cruise? It's a law on cruise ships that you have to have enough little boats attached to the big cruise ship so in case the ship goes down, there are enough little boats for everybody to get on one. Paul stands and says, "God told me to tell you no matter what you have going on, stay on the ship, because nobody on the ship is going down." The enemy wants you to abandon what has brought you this far. For example, you may have been fighting to keep your marriage, fighting to lose weight, fighting to stay celibate, and even fighting to get your finances straight. The reason many people have never gotten to the next level that God has destined for them is because they are holding on to some lifelines. You have got to let them go. Have you ever watched the show Who wants to be a Millionaire? In the show, you have a lifeline which means if you don't have the answer you can always use one of your lifelines. However, there is an issue with lifelines. Lifelines will keep you from trusting in the main line. Have you wondered why God has gotten some people away from you? Whenever you start trusting people more than God, He will remove them. God is trying to get you to a place where you don't have a Plan B. He's trying to get you to a place that if He doesn't help you then there is no help. He is trying to get you to what I call a Shadrach, Meshach, and Abednego thinking. The thinking that says even if God doesn't deliver us, He's still God. Sometimes, God will remove everybody out of your life that you have been leaning on so that when He blesses you, no one can take the credit or praise but God.

God is about to do something in your life that's going to blow your mind! You have to stay on the ship! Your ship might be your family, but stay on the ship! Your ship may be your marriage, but stay on the ship! Your ship may be your church, ministry, or occupation, but stay on the ship! Your ship might be hard and rough at times and it seems like there is no better way, but stay on the ship! Sometimes, you are depressed, but stay on the ship! It hurts, but stay on the ship! It gets hard, but stay on the ship! Sometimes, you feel like you don't care anymore and you're not going to make it, but stay on the ship! You have come too far to abandon the ship.

You have to understand that the ship is literally breaking apart while they are on it, but Paul has the audacity to tell everybody to stay on the ship. Experienced sailors are saying, "We need to abandon the ship now." Meanwhile, Paul is standing there saying, "I've got a Word - stay on the ship." Your ship may be breaking and falling apart and you want to get off the ship to get into one of the little boats because it looks better, but the little boat is not better because God's hand is not on the little boat. God has His hand on your ship. God has angels watching over your ship. It seems like your ship is breaking, but nobody is going to die if you stay on the ship.

Release the Little Boats

Remember the text in Romans Chapter 27. The passengers on the ship were not Christians. In verse 32 (paraphrased) they said, "Okay Paul you heard from God." Paul says, "Cut every boat off the side of the ship and let them float away, because God says, it is either all of Me or none of Me." In perspective, as long as you have those little boats, they are your security blanket. So, the question becomes what or who is your little boat? There is no Plan B and no second option with God. For instance, a believer may say they trust God with their singleness but they have this "friend" on the side, or they play the lottery just in case their tithes don't work. Sometimes, we use our past as a little boat. In Malachi 3:10 (KJV) God says, *"prove me now herewith, saith the Lord of hosts if I will not open you the windows of heaven, and pour you out a blessing, that there shall not be room enough to receive it"* as it relates to tithing. God is putting you in position where you must trust Him and Him alone.

The last scripture I want to look at is Acts 27:34-38 which says, *"'Therefore I encourage you to take some food, for this is for your preservation, for not a hair from the head of any of you will perish.' Having said this, he took bread and gave thanks to God in the presence of all, and he broke it and began to eat. All of them were encouraged and they themselves also took food. All of us in the ship were two hundred and seventy-six persons. When they had eaten enough, they began to lighten the ship by throwing out the wheat into the sea."*

You're Coming Out!

Paul took some bread, broke it, gave thanks, and started to eat. The passengers on the boat were so scared and had not eaten in 14 days. Paul sits down and says (paraphrased), "Y'all better eat; the Lord has got this ship." The Bible says that they looked at Paul and said, "If you can eat in the midst of this, then we are going to eat too." This is why you have to pray and praise God in the bad times. This is why you don't critique anyone else's praise because you don't know what they have gone through. Praise God on your job when everyone else is worried about being laid off. If you panic, your family will panic. Instead, start blessing God in the midst of whatever you're going through. I want to encourage you that you will not lose your house, your marriage will not break up, cancer will not kill you, and depression will not have you. Don't get off the ship no matter who jumps off or who walks away. Sometimes, the ship is rocky, but stay on the ship! In the end, Paul and the other passengers (prisoners and sailors) made it to Rome.

It's now your season to come out of what you have been through. Shout, "I'm coming out!" Better is coming for you - better jobs, raises, bonuses, benefits, sales, settlements, estates, inheritance, interest, income, money on the ground, rebates, returns, checks in the mail, gifts, surprises, bills paid off, debts eliminated, royalties received, more than enough, abundance, and overflow. Shout right now and believe by saying, "That's for me! I receive it in Jesus' name! I am not going to give up; I am going to stay on the ship!" Don't give up on the ship, don't give up on your faith, don't give up on God, and don't give up on your vision. God is about to add His super to your natural, and whatever you are praying for, know it's done. Thank you, Jesus!

Chapter Eleven
You Can't Die, You Must Survive This!

Chapter Twelve
Get Rid of the Weights

Therefore, since we are surrounded by such a great cloud of witnesses, let us throw off everything that hinders and the sin that so easily entangles. And let us run with perseverance the race marked out for us.

Hebrews 12:1 (NIV)

As we come to the last chapter of this book "So Goes the Man, So Goes the Family," as a man, what is your plan or strategy? How are you going to change your spending habits? You need another plan other than "Jesus, help me out of this." Remember that Jesus helps those who help themselves. Rita Mae Brown, an American writer said, "Insanity is doing the same thing the same way expecting different results." Albert Einstein said, "The difference between stupidity and genius is that genius has its limits." So, you have to have a plan for change. As fathers, there are some issues and cycles that we have to break. They are called strongholds. A stronghold is a mindset impregnated with impossibilities. It's when you are in a place where you don't believe you can get delivered.

There are people in our life that God doesn't want there. You have to be clear on this because your assignment in Christ is too important. You cannot have individuals in your life pulling you from your assignment. If they are in your life and all they do is make you feel bad and bring you hurt and disappointment, I'm not sure that God put them in your life. The verse says, "lay aside every weight and the sin." For instance, it may not be a sin to hang out with some people you are associated with but it's a weight. They are pulling you down. They are not helping you to get to the next level. Aren't you tired of dragging people around? What and/or who in your life is a weight as it relates to your spiritual growth? Galatians 5:17 says, *"For the flesh sets its desire against the Spirit, and the Spirit against the flesh; for these are in opposition to one another, so that you may not do the things that you please."*

The flesh and the Spirit oppose one another.

There is a dualistic tension happening in every believer at all times. The Spirit and the flesh are always conflicting. Everyday when you wake up, there is a war going on inside of you. It happens every day. Your flesh wants one thing, and your spirit wants something else. They oppose one another. The question becomes, who's going to win? Those of us that feed our spirit man will prevail. If you feed your Spirit man, he is the strongest. It's great that you go to church twice a week, but what would happen if you ate food twice a week and the other five days, you didn't eat? It would reflect in your physical man. Thank God for the Word that you do receive at the local church you attend, but that cannot be the totality of your spirituality. You have to feed yourself seven days a week.

It's Just a Preview

Now the works of the flesh are evident: sexual immorality, impurity, sensuality, idolatry, sorcery, enmity, strife, jealousy, fits of anger, rivalries, dissensions, divisions, envy, drunkenness, orgies, and things like these. I warn you, as I warned you before, that those who do such things will not inherit the kingdom of God.

Galatians 5:19-21 (ESV)

You should ask yourself: What are some of the demonic things that Satan has in my home that I don't realize is there? I'm going to give you the first one, and it's so deep that I'm going to give it to you in Greek, Hebrew, and Aramaic. This is so deep and I really want you to catch it. It's called TV and interpreted it's called TV. Do you realize the damage that a TV can do when it's not monitored? It's not always about being deep, but sometimes, it's about practical things that are hurting our homes. The enemy has infiltrated basically every home in America with this demonic box that has up to 500 channels or more. Out of all of these choices, only a small amount of those channels have religious overtones. The rest of them are blatantly demonic, and we know it. "Bishop, I watch ESPN." Well, half-naked women are in most of the commercials. Never fall for the preview. The preview means it's coming soon. They show you a clip and you're like, "Wow!", but they only show you 60 seconds of it. Here's what they don't tell you in the preview:

- ◆ It's going to cost you $10.00 to get in.

- It's another $30.00 if you take your family.
- The large drink is going to cost you $19.00.
- The preview was the best part in the movie, and the rest of it isn't worth watching.

So, did you fall for the preview? Be careful because that's just what the devil wants. For men, if a woman walks by with a nice shape, that's just a preview. She can't cook, her breath smells, she's evil, and she doesn't know Jesus. It's just a preview. Don't get it twisted!

TV Addiction

Let's find out if you're a "teleholic"—a TV-holic. Here are some signs:

- You consistently watch TV late into the night.
- When company visits, the TV stays on.
- You disturb others on the job by discussing TV with them.
- You yell if anyone is talking while you're watching TV. You say things like, "My show is on, be quiet!"
- You have thrown things at your children.
- The only book you read is the TV guide.
- You turn the TV on the moment you enter the room.
- The TV is on while you're doing your chores.
- You don't want people to visit while certain programs are on.

- When people do visit, you wish they would leave so that you can watch your favorite program.

It gets more serious here:

- You laugh at the very thing that sent Christ to the cross.
- You are consistently flipping through channels with your remote control.
- You will spend 20 minutes looking for your remote when you could have walked right up to the TV to turn it on.
- You find more pleasure watching TV than being with God's people.

There are consequences of being a "teleholic." First, there is loneliness. Staying home and watching TV isolates you from other people. God created us to be social creatures and loss of human contact can cause extreme loneliness. Excessive TV watching may cause depression because night after night, you continue to soak up the world's ideas of what success and prosperity is. We are allowing our children to watch these videos that promote sex, violence, and money.

Watching too much TV can also cause physical disease because our bodies were made for movement. Some people are depressed, and they just sit in front of the TV all day. Our muscles and our bodies need to exercise to help stimulate and clear our minds. If you're watching TV, then there's a strong chance that you're going to eat, which can then lead to obesity.

Taking Authority over Your Life

Do not bring a detestable thing into your house or you, like it, will be set apart for destruction. Regard it as vile and utterly detest it, for it is set apart for destruction.

Deuteronomy 7:26 (NIV)

Some people have things in their house that invite demons in. What's in your house? I'm not trying to be overly spooky like everything must have a picture of Jesus on it. You may have pictures of some people that you need to let go. Why are you keeping pictures? You ought to go in your backyard and burn those as a peace offering. There are certain records, CDs, and music that need to go. For example, why do you still have, "Me and Mrs. Jones"? It sounds great, but the song is talking about adultery. Every song that sounds great is not necessarily good for your spirit. The Bible says in Second Corinthians 5:17 (NKJV), *"Therefore if anyone is in Christ, he is a new creation; old things have passed away; behold, all things have become new."* Go home, find out what's in your house, and take inventory.

Finally, you have to be careful with your cell phone. First, you need to delete and throw away certain phone numbers for good. The enemy makes you think that you have to have a cell phone, which means people have access to you anytime. In 1984, we didn't think about a cell phone. Now, we will drive back home 20 miles away to get our cell phone. The Bible says to be careful and not to fill your ear with filthy communication. Colossians 3:8 (NIV) says, *"But now you must also rid yourselves of all such things as these: anger, rage, malice, slander, and filthy language from your lips."* To concur with this, Ephesians 4:29 says, *"Let no unwholesome word proceed from your mouth, but only such a word as is good for edification according to the need of the moment, so that it will give grace to those who hear."* The wrong people will take you away from God.

Chapter Twelve
Get Rid of the Weights

So Goes the Woman

Reflections by Pastor Anita F. Jackson

So Goes the Woman　　　　　**Chapter Ten**

Raise Your Level of Expectation

Let me tell you what I know. Bishop Getties L. Jackson, Sr. is a true man of God. He is a Kingdom man, and he walks in Kingdom authority. He truly has a heart for men. I live with Bishop, and I know his walk so this is very real and personal for me. I watch him speak into the lives of fathers and sons. I see him affirming their identity in Christ; that they are the priest, prophet, and king of their home. I see him helping men to reach their full potential. In July 1985, I watched my husband in his most painful and difficult times in his life when God was in the process of breaking him in order to prepare him for greater service. It was very hard, but look at God! God was preparing him for ministry for the family; for the whole family and especially men. Philippians 1:6 is Bishop's life verse. I know that to be true in his life. God will complete what He has started in our lives.

On pages 146 and 147, Bishop talked about changing your thinking. As a stay-at-home mother when our children were small, I watched Bishop change his thinking. He received his Bachelor of Arts in Theology from Emanuel Baptist University and his Master of Divinity from Gardner Webb University. Bishop was able to complete some things in order for our family to go further in ministry. God has been so good to us. When we change our thought life and do a Matthew 6:33, God will do the rest.

So Goes the Woman   # Chapter Eleven
You Can't Die, You Must Survive This!

God is telling us as believers, like Paul, we will survive the storm. God said to be of good cheer. He said to cast all of our anxiety on Him [Christ] because He cares for us (I Peter 5:7). Bishop and I have stayed on the ship through the storm. You may look at your life and wonder, "God, how did I get in this mess? Why did you allow me to fall into this place? How will I ever get out of this?" Remember, storms may (and will) come, but stay on the ship. Remember Hebrews 13:5 (NKJV), *"For He Himself has said, 'I will never leave you nor forsake you.'"*

So Goes the Woman   # Chapter Twelve
Get Rid of the Weights!

Bishop asked the question, "As a man, what is your plan or strategy?" Many times, I have heard him say, "If you fail to plan, you plan to fail." Men of God, as the priest, prophet, and king of your family, you are the one to plan and to lead your family in Kingdom principles. You are the one who, with your plan and strategy, will break the generational curses. You have to be the one who stands up and says, "As for me and my house ..." If there is anything or anyone hindering you from walking in your purpose or in your assignment, now is the time to get rid of the weight. You may think it is difficult to do, but you can do all things though Christ who strengthens you. You are more than a conqueror through Him.

In closing, I am so glad to have had the opportunity to write words of encouragement in my husband's book So Goes the Man, So Goes the Family. Bishop and I have been married for 32 years. We have seen good times, and we have seen some not so good times. I am able to say and encourage every married person, every single person, and to the young generation to "Trust in our Lord and Savior, Jesus Christ!" Colossians 1:17 (NKJV) tells us *"And He is before all things, and in Him all things consist"*, and Acts 17:28 (NKJV) tells us *"for in Him we live and move and have our being."*

Pastor Anita F. Jackson
Luke 9:23

1. The song, "Nothing but the Blood of Jesus" by Robert Lowry (1876)

2. The song, "The Blood Will Never Loose Its Power" by Pastor Andrae Crouch (1962)

3. http://www.city-journal.org/html/15_3_black_family.html

4. BibleGateway, https://www.biblegateway.com/

5. http://www.ap.org/

6. http://www.allaboutdepression.com/gen_01.html

7. http://www.cruising.org/regulatory/issues-facts/passenger-safety-security/ship-safety

8. http://en.wikipedia.org/wiki/Who_Wants_to_Be_a_Millionaire_%28U.S._game_show%29

9. The song, "The World Didn't Give It To Me" by Pastor Shirley Caesar from the album *Be Careful of the Stones You Throw* (1975)

10. The Song, "Me and Mrs. Jones" by Billy Paul from the album *360 Degrees of Billy Paul* (1972)

11. The Brown-Driver Briggs, Hebrew and English Lexicon

12. Nelson's Illustrated Bible Dictionary

13. Greek-English Lexicon of the New Testament 2nd Edition: Walter Bauer's

14. Gilder, G.F. *Sexual Suicide*. Quadrangle, 1973.

15. http://bodyecology.com/articles/top-5-sources-of-toxins.php

16. http://www.goodreads.com/author/quotes/23511.Rita_Mae_Brown

17. http://www.brainyquote.com/quotes/quotes/a/alberteins148851.html

If you would like to schedule Bishop Getties L. Jackson, Sr., M.Div., as a speaker or facilitator or if you would like more information about Kingdom Assembly Outreach Center and/or Kingdom Assembly Fellowship of Pastors, please contact our office via the following contact info:

churchoffice@kingdomaoc.com

www.kingdomaoc.com

(864) 655-5990 (Office)

Kingdom Assembly Outreach Center

P.O. Box 1273

Greer, SC 29652

Bishop Getties L. Jackson, Sr. is devoted to promoting a clear understanding and relevant application of Scripture in order to bring about changes in urban communities by teaching Kingdom of God principles in a way that even a child can understand. Bishop Jackson is chosen by the Lord to bring forth a vision through Kingdom Assembly Outreach Center. He is the founding Senior Pastor of Kingdom Assembly Outreach Center, which began in March of 1997. Under Bishop Jackson's leadership, the church continues to grow with a flourishing and healthy membership. Kingdom Assembly Outreach Center is blessed to have a Teen Center, Fitness Center, and a Kingdom Bookstore along with administrative offices.

Bishop Jackson was married to Mrs. De'Anita Frye Jackson on January 29, 1983. They have one son and two daughters: Getties Jr., Angelica, and Crystal. They have two Grandsons: Edward Jay-Lee Hill and Caden Nathaniel Flemming.

Bishop Jackson is a graduate of Emanuel Bible College with a Bachelor of Arts degree in Theology and a Master of Divinity from M. Christopher White School of Divinity at Gardner Webb University in Christian Education. Bishop Jackson is among the first of five African Americans to receive his Master of Divinity degree from Gardner Webb University (a 100-year old institution) with a strong focus on language proficiency in Greek and Hebrew.

Bishop Jackson is known as an anointed teacher and preacher of the gospel as well as an effective visionary. He is the founder and past executive producer of Urban Contemporary Gospel of

WLFJ Radio in Greenville, South Carolina. Previously, Bishop Jackson served as Chairman of the School Improvement Council at Northwood Middle School. He is a graduate of the Leadership Greer Class of XXVIII and formerly served as a board member of the chamber of commerce. Bishop Jackson's relational attitude has built a strong rapport with local churches and political leaders alike.

Bishop Jackson began preaching August 4, 1985. He is the former pastor of Mt. Nebo Baptist Church of Lake Lure, North Carolina from 1989 to 1993. He also pastored Enoree Fork Baptist Church of Greer, South Carolina from 1993 to 1997.

Bishop Jackson is very focused-driven to fulfill the call of God. He is the author of the books titled: *This Is My Season For Grace and Favor; God's Best For Your Life;* and *So Goes The Man, So Goes The Family.* Bishop Jackson is the Presiding Prelate of Kingdom Assembly Fellowship of Pastors. This senior pastor and spouse fellowship consists of approximately 20 churches from the states of South Carolina, North Carolina, and Georgia.

Made in the USA
Columbia, SC
13 June 2024

36761034R00104